WORLD HISTORY
THE HUMAN EXPERIENCE

Time Line Activities

NATIONAL GEOGRAPHIC SOCIETY

Mounir A. Farah

Andrea Berens Karls

GLENCOE
McGraw-Hill

New York, New York   Columbus, Ohio   Woodland Hills, California   Peoria, Illinois

Customize Your Resources

No matter how you organize your teaching resources, Glencoe has what you need.

The **Teacher's Classroom Resources** for *World History: The Human Experience* provides you with a wide variety of supplemental materials to enhance the classroom experience. These resources appear as individual booklets accompanied by a file management kit of file folders, labels, and tabbed binder dividers in a carryall file box. The booklets are designed to open flat so that pages can be easily photocopied without removing them from their booklets. However, if you choose to create separate files, the pages are perforated for easy removal. You may customize these materials using our file folders or tabbed dividers.

The individual booklets and the file management kit supplied in **Teacher's Classroom Resources** give you the flexibility to organize these resources in a combination that best suits your teaching style. Below are several alternatives:

- **Organize all resources by category**
  (all Tests, all Geography and History Activities, all History Simulations, and so on, filed separately)

- **Organize resources by category and chapter**
  (all Chapter 1 activities, all Chapter 1 tests, etc.)

- **Organize resources sequentially by lesson**
  (activities, quizzes, study guides, etc., for Section 1, Section 2, and so on)

Glencoe/McGraw-Hill
A Division of The McGraw-Hill Companies

Copyright © by the McGraw-Hill Companies, Inc. All rights reserved. Permission is granted to reproduce the material contained herein on the condition that such material be reproduced only for classroom use; be provided to students, teachers, and families without charge; and be used solely in conjunction with *World History: The Human Experience*. Any other reproduction, for use or sale, is prohibited without prior written permission of the publisher.

Send all inquiries to:
Glencoe/McGraw-Hill
936 Eastwind Drive
Westerville, OH 43081

ISBN 0-02-823242-9

Printed in the United States of America
5 6 7 8 9 10   045   02 01 00 99

TIME LINE ACTIVITIES

TABLE OF CONTENTS

To the Teacher		iv
Chapter 1	Human Beginnings	1
Chapter 2	Early Civilizations	2
Chapter 3	Kingdoms and Empires in the Middle East	3
Chapter 4	The Rise of Ancient Greece	4
Chapter 5	The Height of Greek Civilization	5
Chapter 6	Ancient Rome and Early Christianity	6
Chapter 7	Flowering of African Civilizations	7
Chapter 8	India's Great Civilization	8
Chapter 9	China's Flourishing Civilization	9
Chapter 10	Byzantines and Slavs	10
Chapter 11	Islamic Civilization	11
Chapter 12	The Rise of Medieval Europe	12
Chapter 13	Medieval Europe at Its Height	13
Chapter 14	East and South Asia	14
Chapter 15	The Americas	15
Chapter 16	Renaissance and Reformation	16
Chapter 17	Expanding Horizons	17
Chapter 18	Empires of Asia	18
Chapter 19	Royal Power and Conflict	19
Chapter 20	Scientific Revolution	20
Chapter 21	English and American Revolutions	21
Chapter 22	The French Revolution	22
Chapter 23	Age of Industry	23
Chapter 24	Cultural Revolution	24
Chapter 25	Democracy and Reform	25
Chapter 26	Reaction and Nationalism	26
Chapter 27	The Age of Imperialism	27
Chapter 28	World War I	28
Chapter 29	Between Two Fires	29
Chapter 30	Nationalism in Asia, Africa, and Latin America	30
Chapter 31	World War II	31
Chapter 32	The Cold War	32
Chapter 33	Asia and the Pacific	33
Chapter 34	Africa	34
Chapter 35	The Middle East	35
Chapter 36	Latin America	36
Chapter 37	The World in Transition	37
Answer Key		38

To the Teacher

Time Line Activities are designed to help students learn the chronological order of historical events and the dates on which those events occurred. Each activity provides dates and events marked on a time line, and asks questions about this information. This activity can be used to preteach the chapters or to review them in preparation for section quizzes and chapter tests.

Answers to the activities are provided at the back of the booklet.

Name .... Date .... Class ....

Time Line Activity 1

Human Beginnings

Look at the events listed on the time line below. Write each event in the box next to the concept to which it relates. Then give a reason why the event is related to the concept. (Events may be related to more than one concept.)

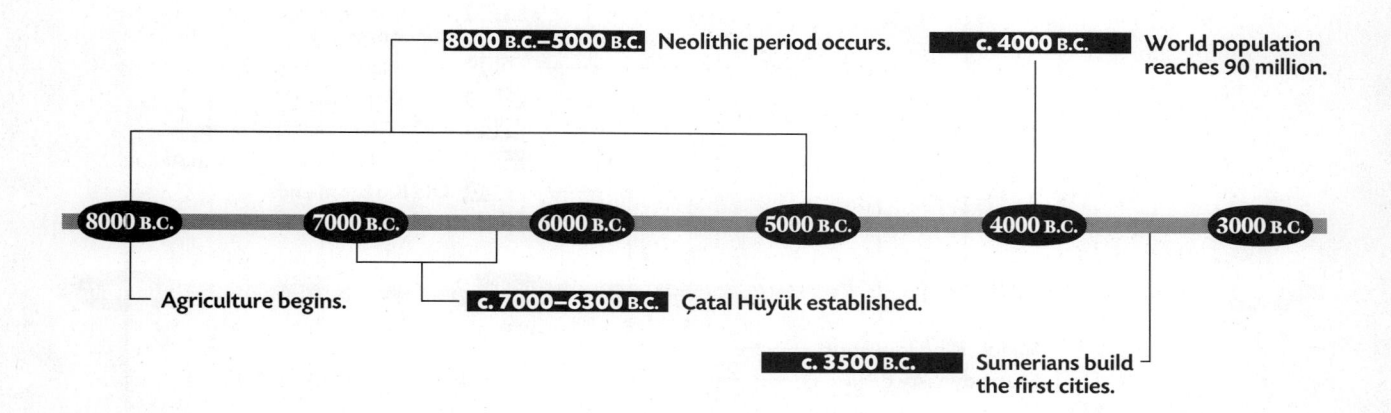

8000 B.C.–5000 B.C. Neolithic period occurs.

c. 4000 B.C. World population reaches 90 million.

8000 B.C. — 7000 B.C. — 6000 B.C. — 5000 B.C. — 4000 B.C. — 3000 B.C.

Agriculture begins.

c. 7000–6300 B.C. Çatal Hüyük established.

c. 3500 B.C. Sumerians build the first cities.

Concept	Event	Reason
Technology		
Domestication		
Civilization		

World History — Time Line Activities — **1**

Name _____ Date _____ Class _____

Time Line Activity 2

Early Civilizations

The ancient civilizations of Egypt, Mesopotamia, India, and China covered a period of 3,000 years. Use the time line below to complete the sentences or answer the questions that follow.

3100 Sumerians invent cuneiform.
3000 King Narmer unites Egypt.
2700 Old Kingdom begins.
2500 Indus River civilization begins.
2300 Sargon I assumes power in Akkad.
2200 Old Kingdom ends.
2050 Middle Kingdom begins.

4000 B.C. — 3000 B.C. — 2000 B.C. — 1000 B.C.

1800 Middle Kingdom ends.
1700 Shang dynasty begins.
1600 New Kingdom begins.
1480 Queen Hatshepsut comes to power.
1200 Rule of Ramses II begins.
1000 Shang dynasty ends. Zhou dynasty begins.

1. The Shang dynasty began in _____ and ended in _____ .
2. Sargon I assumed power in Akkad in _____ .
3. During which kingdom did Queen Hatshepsut come to power? _____
4. Which is older, the Indus River valley civilization or the Middle Kingdom of Egypt? _____
5. King Narmer united Egypt in _____ .
6. The Zhou dynasty began in _____ .
7. How many years did the Old Kingdom last? _____
8. How many years are there between the beginning of the Old Kingdom and the beginning of the New Kingdom? _____
9. Cuneiform was invented in _____ .
10. How many years separate the rule of King Narmer from the rule of Ramses II? _____

Name _____ Date _____ Class _____

Time Line Activity 3

Kingdoms and Empires in the Middle East

The traders, Israelites, and conquerors who lived in the Middle East in ancient times greatly shaped the development of the region. In addition, these early cultures had a profound influence on our modern lives. Analyze the following time line to discover more about the cultures of the ancient Middle East and their influence.

1900 B.C. Abraham makes a covenant with God; monotheism created.
1200 B.C. Aramaeans control rich overland trade between Egypt and Mesopotamia.

Timeline: 2000 B.C. — 1600 B.C. — 1200 B.C. — 800 B.C. — 400 B.C.

1100 B.C. Phoenician traders take charge of Mediterranean shipping and trading, colonizing the Mediterranean.
1000 B.C. Phoenicians develop a simplified alphabet.
922 B.C. Ten northern Israelite tribes break away from two southern tribes.
722 B.C. Assyrians conquer Israel.
650 B.C. Assyrian Empire reaches its height.
600 B.C. Lydians develop a money system using coins.
486 B.C. Persian ruler Darius I dies.

Analyzing the Time Line

Study the events shown on the time line above. On a separate sheet of paper, make a chart similar to the one below. In it, write each event next to the concept to which it is linked. Then explain how the event and concept are connected. Some events may be linked to more than one concept.

Concept	Event	Explanation
Cultural Diffusion	Phoenician traders take charge of Mediterranean shipping and trading, colonizing the Mediterranean.	Phoenicians spread their simplified alphabet throughout the region.
Innovation		
Conflict		

World History Time Line Activities **3**

Name .... Date .... Class ....

Time Line Activity 4

The Rise of Ancient Greece

The complex history of Greek civilization spans nearly 2,500 years. The time line below charts some of the main events in this long process. Read Chapter 4 and this time line, then answer the questions below.

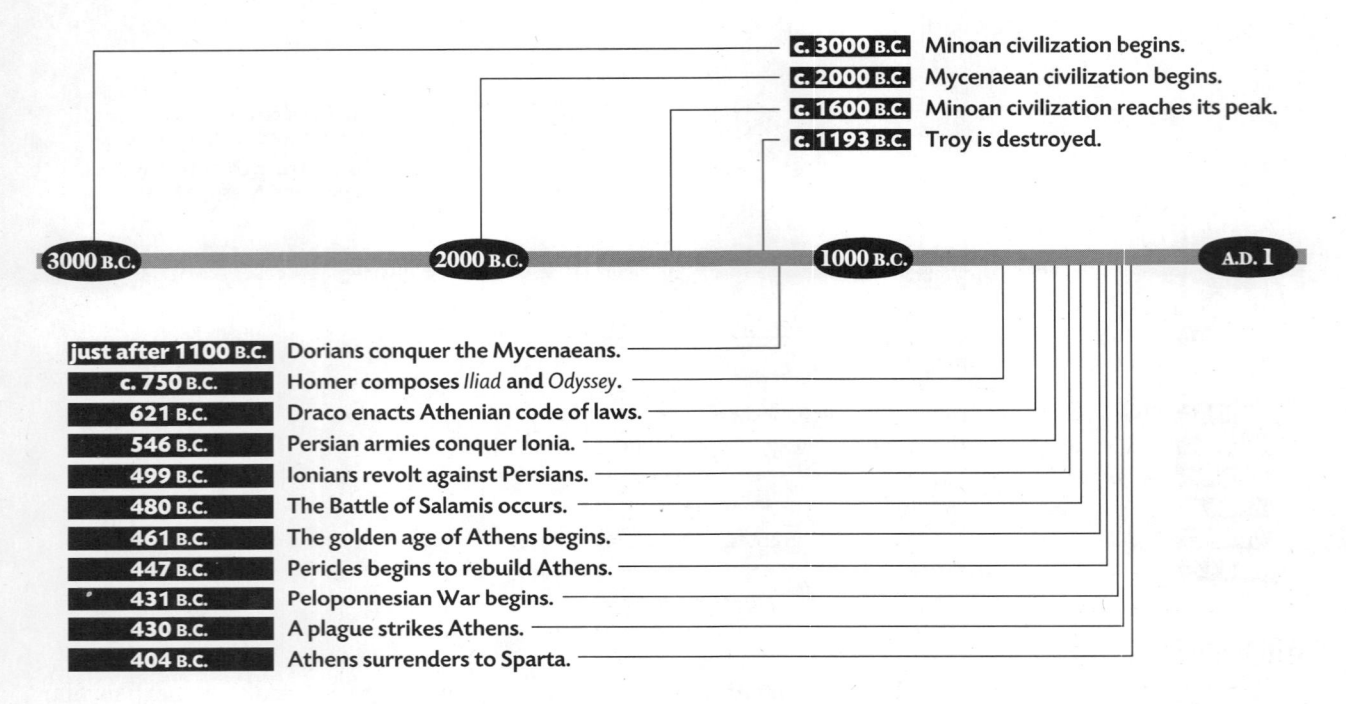

c. 3000 B.C.	Minoan civilization begins.
c. 2000 B.C.	Mycenaean civilization begins.
c. 1600 B.C.	Minoan civilization reaches its peak.
c. 1193 B.C.	Troy is destroyed.
just after 1100 B.C.	Dorians conquer the Mycenaeans.
c. 750 B.C.	Homer composes *Iliad* and *Odyssey*.
621 B.C.	Draco enacts Athenian code of laws.
546 B.C.	Persian armies conquer Ionia.
499 B.C.	Ionians revolt against Persians.
480 B.C.	The Battle of Salamis occurs.
461 B.C.	The golden age of Athens begins.
447 B.C.	Pericles begins to rebuild Athens.
431 B.C.	Peloponnesian War begins.
430 B.C.	A plague strikes Athens.
404 B.C.	Athens surrenders to Sparta.

1. The "c." on the time line means *circa*, or approximately. Why do you think the earliest entries on the time line are estimated, not exact, dates?

2. How much time elapsed between the fall of Troy and Homer's account of the Trojan War?

3. When did the ancestors of the Spartans first enter into Greece?

4. When did tyrants begin to rule Athens?

5. How much time passed between the end of the Persian War and Pericles' rebuilding of Athens?

Name .... Date .... Class ....

Time Line Activity 5

The Height of Greek Civilization

From the beginning of the Golden Age of Athens in the mid-400s B.C. to the death of Alexander in 323 B.C., Greek civilization reached its height. The time line below charts some of the main events in this important time in Greece's history. Read the time line, then answer the questions that follow.

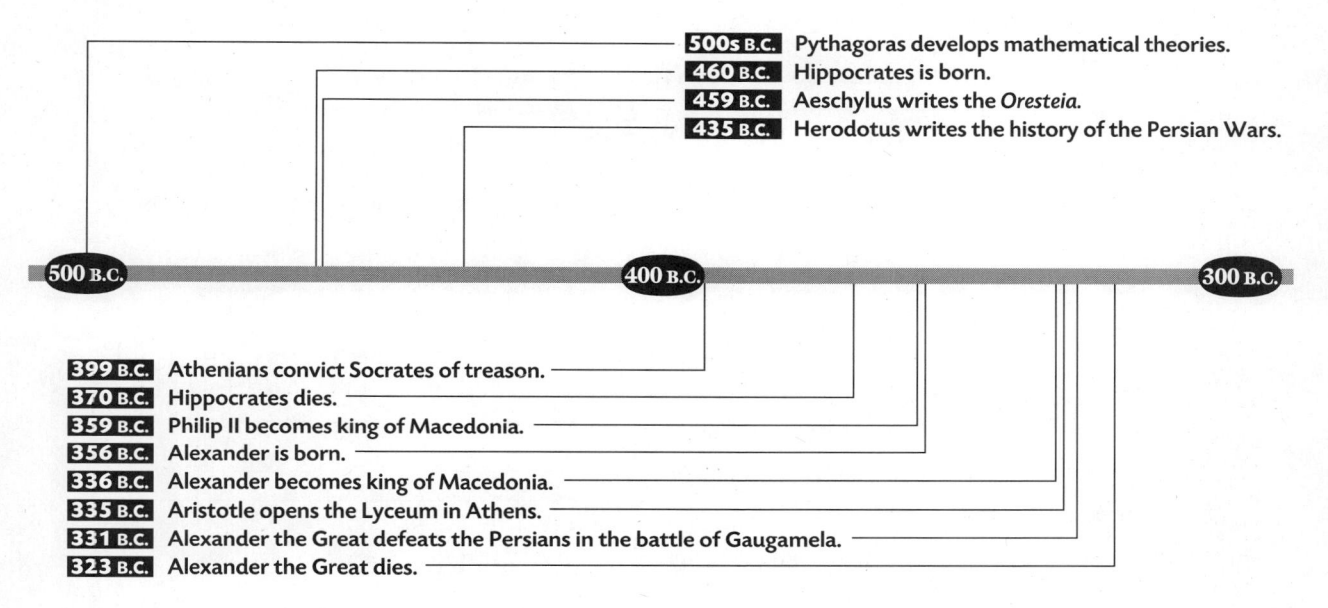

500s B.C. Pythagoras develops mathematical theories.
460 B.C. Hippocrates is born.
459 B.C. Aeschylus writes the *Oresteia*.
435 B.C. Herodotus writes the history of the Persian Wars.

500 B.C. ———————————— 400 B.C. ———————————— 300 B.C.

399 B.C. Athenians convict Socrates of treason.
370 B.C. Hippocrates dies.
359 B.C. Philip II becomes king of Macedonia.
356 B.C. Alexander is born.
336 B.C. Alexander becomes king of Macedonia.
335 B.C. Aristotle opens the Lyceum in Athens.
331 B.C. Alexander the Great defeats the Persians in the battle of Gaugamela.
323 B.C. Alexander the Great dies.

1. How much time elapsed between the writing of the *Oresteia* and the writing of the *Historia*? _____

2. Which spanned more time: Philip II's reign or Alexander the Great's reign? _____

3. Who lived longer, Hippocrates or Alexander? _____

4. Which occurred first, the battle of Gaugamela or the opening of the Lyceum? _____

5. Who died later, Socrates or Hippocrates? _____

World History — Time Line Activities — 5

Name _____ Date _____ Class _____

Time Line Activity 6

Ancient Rome and Early Christianity

The Roman Republic and the Roman Empire each lasted about 500 years. The time line below shows some of the major events of this 1,000-year period. Study the time line to decide whether the statements that follow are true or false. Mark each answer T for true, or F for false, then explain your answer on the line below the statement.

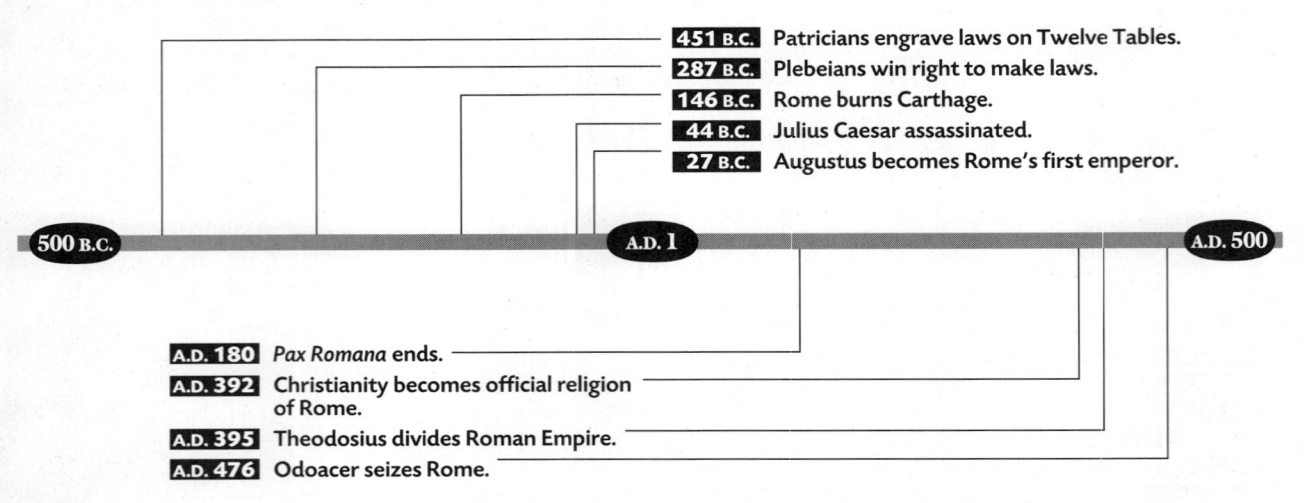

451 B.C. Patricians engrave laws on Twelve Tables.
287 B.C. Plebeians win right to make laws.
146 B.C. Rome burns Carthage.
44 B.C. Julius Caesar assassinated.
27 B.C. Augustus becomes Rome's first emperor.

500 B.C. ——————————— A.D. 1 ——————————— A.D. 500

A.D. 180 Pax Romana ends.
A.D. 392 Christianity becomes official religion of Rome.
A.D. 395 Theodosius divides Roman Empire.
A.D. 476 Odoacer seizes Rome.

1. Plebeians had more power than patricians in the early Roman Republic.
_____

2. As Rome became more democratic, it also developed peaceful relations with Carthage.
_____

3. Julius Caesar came to power after Rome defeated Carthage.
_____

4. Julius Caesar was Rome's first emperor.
_____

5. The *Pax Romana*, which began when Augustus took power, lasted about 200 years.
_____

6. Christianity became the official religion of Rome about 350 years after the death of Jesus.
_____

6 Time Line Activities   World History

Name _____ Date _____ Class _____

Time Line Activity 7

Flowering of African Civilizations

Much of Africa's history was driven by the availability of resources and trade. Contact between civilizations often resulted in the conquest of one over another. Read the time line below, then answer the questions that follow.

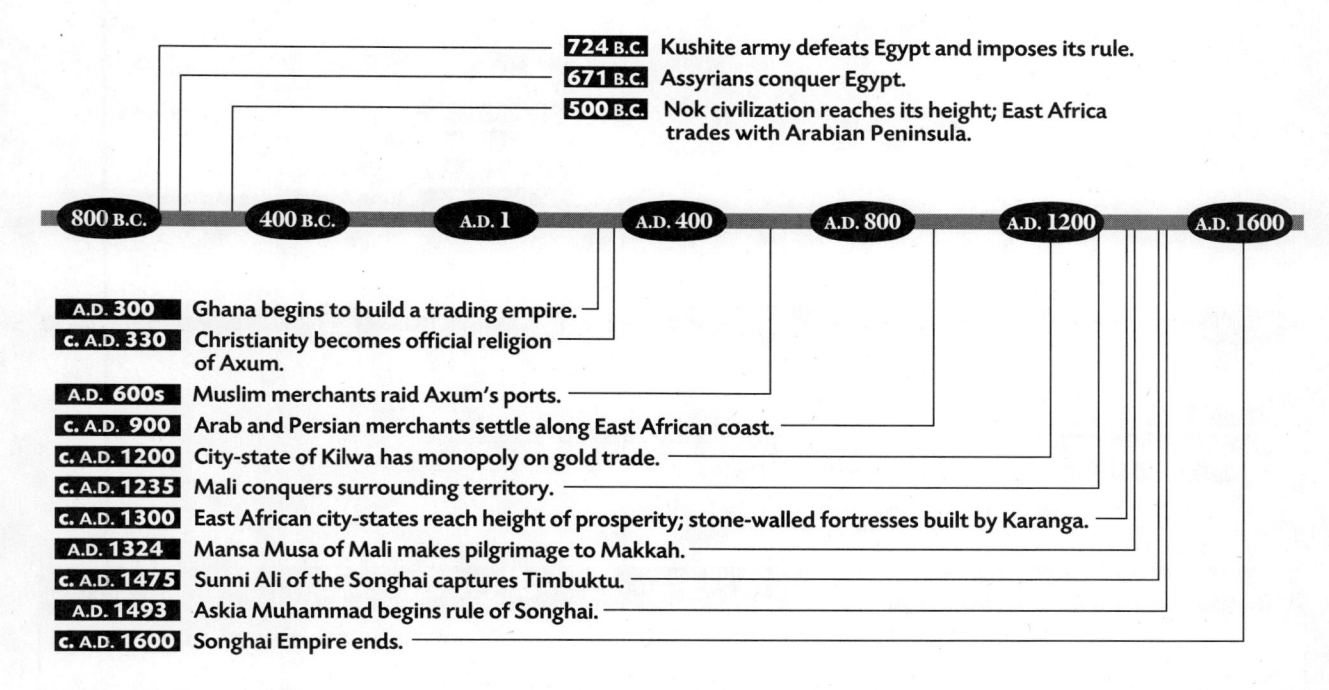

724 B.C. Kushite army defeats Egypt and imposes its rule.
671 B.C. Assyrians conquer Egypt.
500 B.C. Nok civilization reaches its height; East Africa trades with Arabian Peninsula.

800 B.C. — 400 B.C. — A.D. 1 — A.D. 400 — A.D. 800 — A.D. 1200 — A.D. 1600

A.D. 300 Ghana begins to build a trading empire.
c. A.D. 330 Christianity becomes official religion of Axum.
A.D. 600s Muslim merchants raid Axum's ports.
c. A.D. 900 Arab and Persian merchants settle along East African coast.
c. A.D. 1200 City-state of Kilwa has monopoly on gold trade.
c. A.D. 1235 Mali conquers surrounding territory.
c. A.D. 1300 East African city-states reach height of prosperity; stone-walled fortresses built by Karanga.
A.D. 1324 Mansa Musa of Mali makes pilgrimage to Makkah.
c. A.D. 1475 Sunni Ali of the Songhai captures Timbuktu.
A.D. 1493 Askia Muhammad begins rule of Songhai.
c. A.D. 1600 Songhai Empire ends.

1. The kingdom of Mali eventually conquered the kingdom of Ghana's territory. About how long did the kingdom of Ghana last? _____

2. When did East Africa begin trading with merchants from the Arabian Peninsula? _____

3. How long did Kushite rule over Egypt last? _____

4. About what year was Islam introduced to Mali? _____

5. What change took place in Axum during the fourth century A.D.?
_____

6. When did the Songhai Empire begin? _____

7. Ghana existed at the time of what other kingdom? _____

8. What cultural change occurred in Africa beginning in the tenth century A.D.?
_____

World History   Time Line Activities   7

Name .... Date .... Class ....

Time Line Activity 8

India's Great Civilization

The time line below shows major events in India's early history. List each event next to the concept in the table it represents, caused, or resulted from. Then tell why you think that concept makes the event significant in Indian history. Some events may fit into more than one category. An example has been done for you.

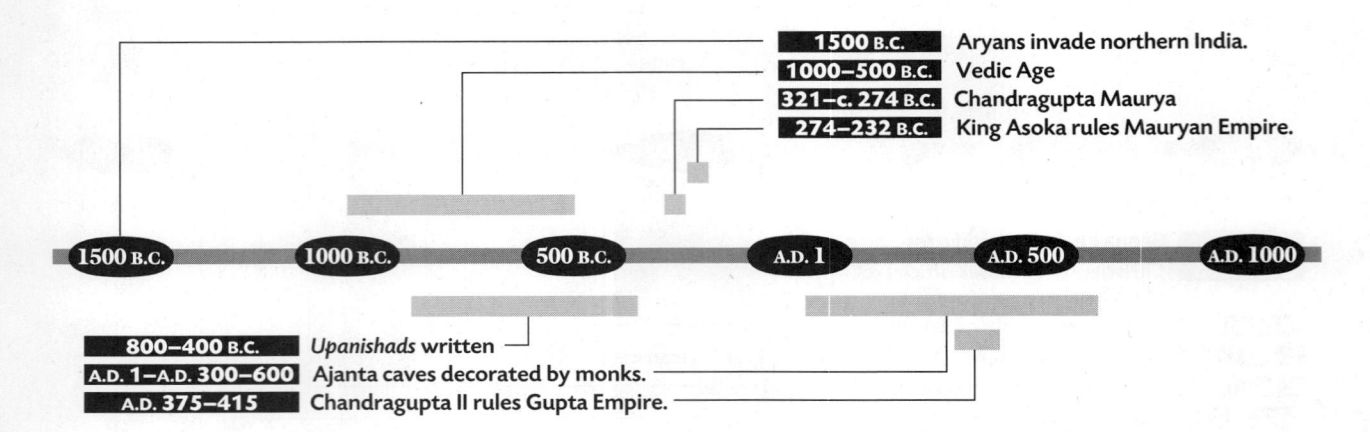

1500 B.C. Aryans invade northern India.
1000–500 B.C. Vedic Age
321–c. 274 B.C. Chandragupta Maurya
274–232 B.C. King Asoka rules Mauryan Empire.

1500 B.C. — 1000 B.C. — 500 B.C. — A.D. 1 — A.D. 500 — A.D. 1000

800–400 B.C. *Upanishads* written
A.D. 1–A.D. 300–600 Ajanta caves decorated by monks.
A.D. 375–415 Chandragupta II rules Gupta Empire.

Concept	Event	Significance
Unity	King Asoka rules Mauryan Empire.	He controlled more than two-thirds of India.
Innovation	King Asoka rules Mauryan Empire.	Asoka believed in religious tolerance and allowed Hindus and Buddhists freedom of worship.
Conflict		

Name .... Date .... Class ....

Time Line Activity 9

China's Flourishing Civilization

Historical eras are often marked by the life spans of powerful rulers or dynasties and are named for these rulers. Such distinctions are useful because they allow historians to analyze trends in culture, politics, and society over a fixed period of time and draw conclusions about how past generations lived. Copy the chart below onto another sheet of paper. For each column, use the time line provided to fill in important information about the three Chinese dynasties listed. Then write a brief description of what life was probably like for an average person living at the time based on the information you have assembled. One example has been partially done for you.

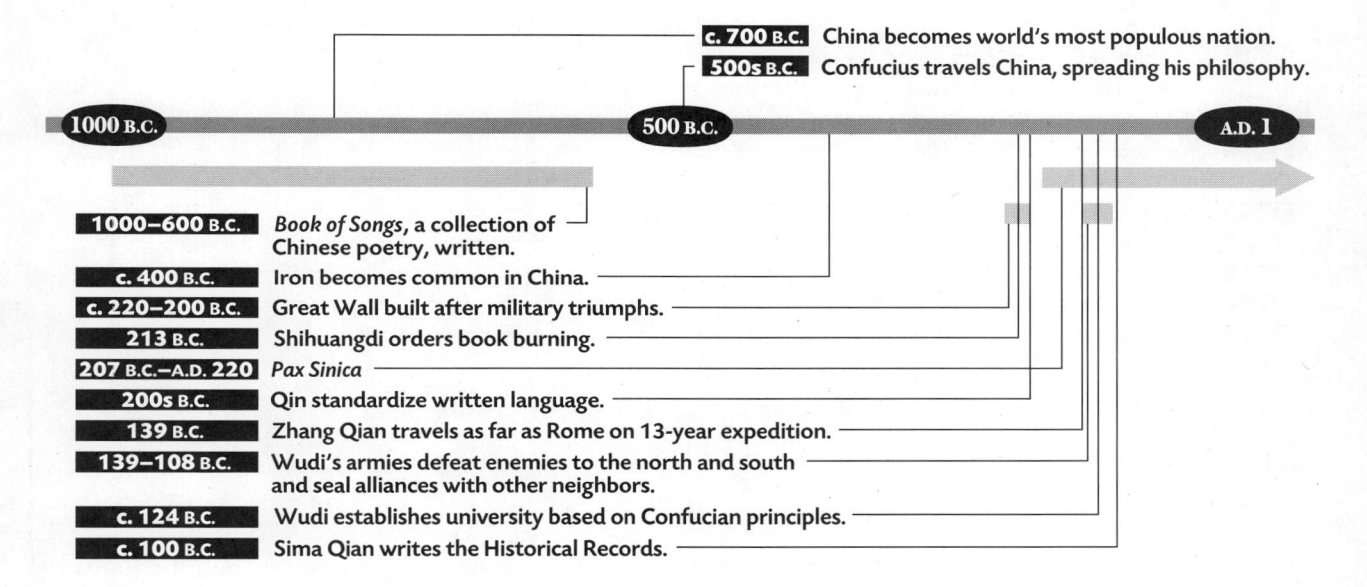

c. 700 B.C. China becomes world's most populous nation.
500s B.C. Confucius travels China, spreading his philosophy.

1000 B.C. ——————— 500 B.C. ——————— A.D. 1

1000–600 B.C. *Book of Songs*, a collection of Chinese poetry, written.
c. 400 B.C. Iron becomes common in China.
c. 220–200 B.C. Great Wall built after military triumphs.
213 B.C. Shihuangdi orders book burning.
207 B.C.–A.D. 220 Pax Sinica
200s B.C. Qin standardize written language.
139 B.C. Zhang Qian travels as far as Rome on 13-year expedition.
139–108 B.C. Wudi's armies defeat enemies to the north and south and seal alliances with other neighbors.
c. 124 B.C. Wudi establishes university based on Confucian principles.
c. 100 B.C. Sima Qian writes the Historical Records.

Dynasty/Ruler	Major Events	Life During Era
Zhou (1028–400s B.C.)	*Book of Songs* written. Iron becomes common in China. China's population exceeds that of other countries.	The introduction of iron tools makes it possible to feed the growing society.
Qin under Shihuangdi (221–207 B.C.)		
Han under Wudi (141–87 B.C.)		

World History   Time Line Activities   **9**

Name _____ Date _____ Class _____

Time Line Activity 10

Byzantines and Slavs

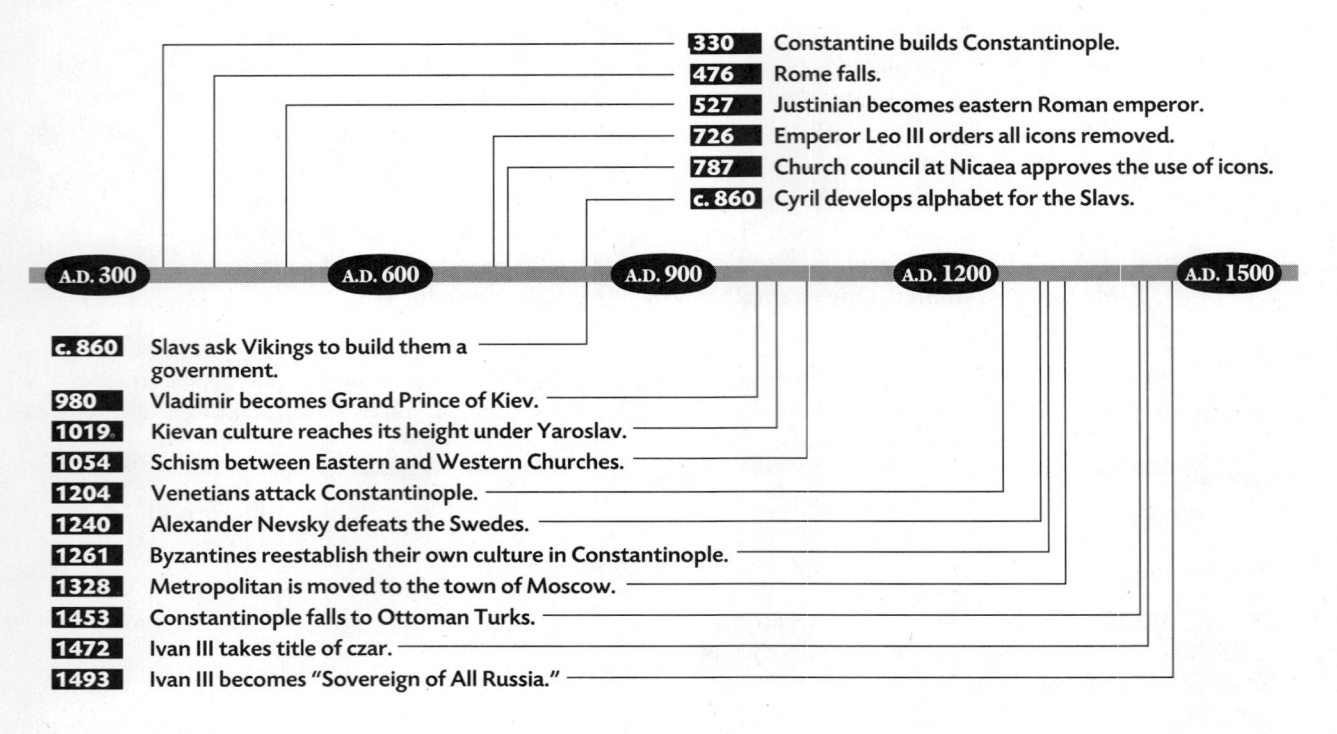

330 Constantine builds Constantinople.
476 Rome falls.
527 Justinian becomes eastern Roman emperor.
726 Emperor Leo III orders all icons removed.
787 Church council at Nicaea approves the use of icons.
c. 860 Cyril develops alphabet for the Slavs.

A.D. 300 — A.D. 600 — A.D. 900 — A.D. 1200 — A.D. 1500

c. 860 Slavs ask Vikings to build them a government.
980 Vladimir becomes Grand Prince of Kiev.
1019 Kievan culture reaches its height under Yaroslav.
1054 Schism between Eastern and Western Churches.
1204 Venetians attack Constantinople.
1240 Alexander Nevsky defeats the Swedes.
1261 Byzantines reestablish their own culture in Constantinople.
1328 Metropolitan is moved to the town of Moscow.
1453 Constantinople falls to Ottoman Turks.
1472 Ivan III takes title of czar.
1493 Ivan III becomes "Sovereign of All Russia."

Look at the events listed on the time line above to answer the following questions.

1. How many years passed between the rise and fall of Constantinople? _____

2. When was the message of the Bible spread to the Slavic peoples? _____

3. After the Venetians and their European allies defeated the Byzantines, they established the Latin empire. When did this change take place? _____

4. How long did the Latin empire last? _____

5. Who led Kievan Rus during its golden age? _____

6. Moscow began as a small town that gradually expanded its control over surrounding territory. About how many years did it take for this town to become the capital of a huge empire? _____

7. When did the iconoclasts achieve their aims? _____

8. When did Rurik, the Viking leader, accept an invitation to rule over the Eastern Slavs?

_____

Name _____ Date _____ Class _____

Time Line Activity 11

Islamic Civilization

The first centuries of Islamic civilization were a time of expansion and accomplishment. Read the time line below, then answer the questions that follow.

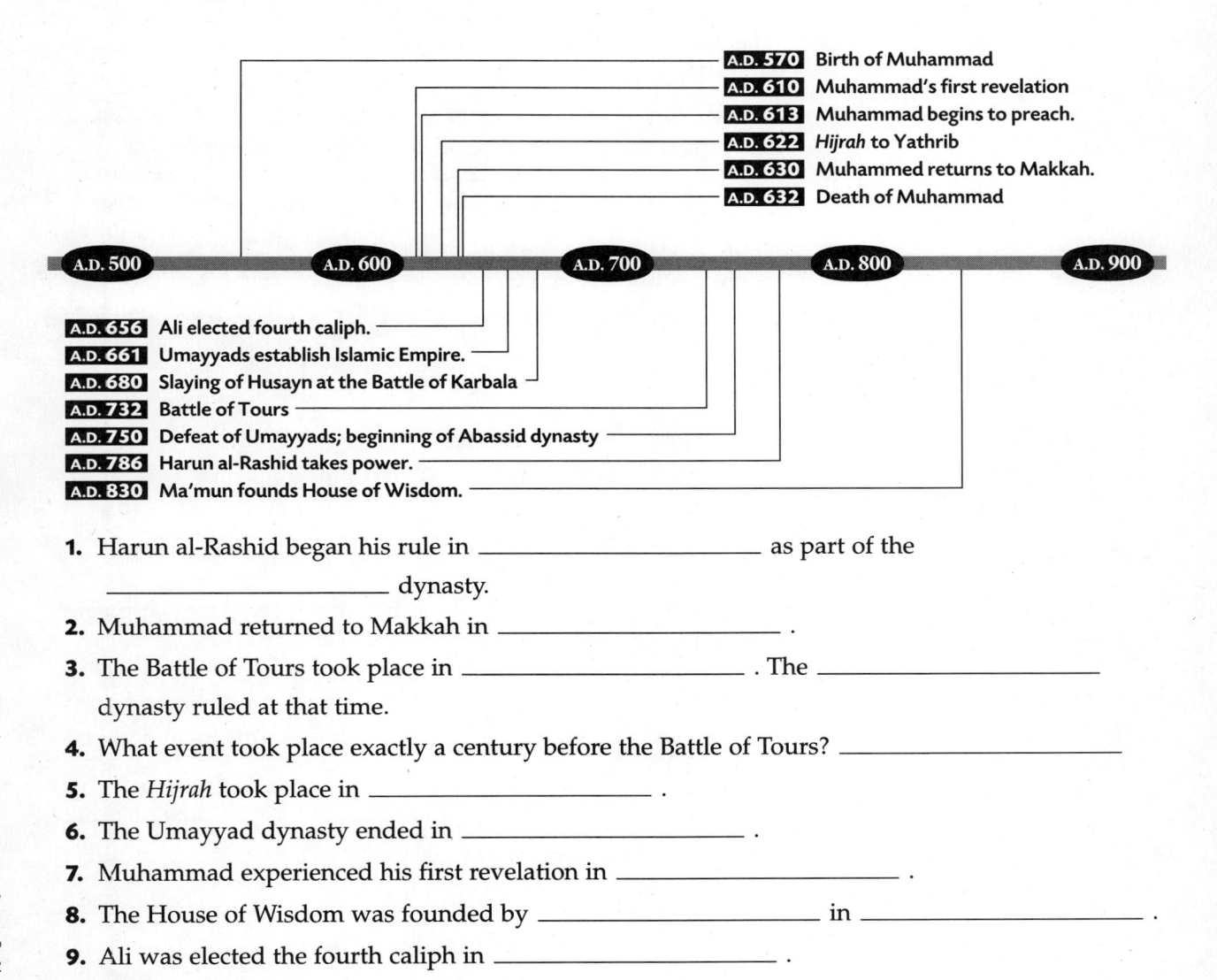

A.D. 570 Birth of Muhammad
A.D. 610 Muhammad's first revelation
A.D. 613 Muhammad begins to preach.
A.D. 622 *Hijrah* to Yathrib
A.D. 630 Muhammed returns to Makkah.
A.D. 632 Death of Muhammad

A.D. 500 — A.D. 600 — A.D. 700 — A.D. 800 — A.D. 900

A.D. 656 Ali elected fourth caliph.
A.D. 661 Umayyads establish Islamic Empire.
A.D. 680 Slaying of Husayn at the Battle of Karbala
A.D. 732 Battle of Tours
A.D. 750 Defeat of Umayyads; beginning of Abassid dynasty
A.D. 786 Harun al-Rashid takes power.
A.D. 830 Ma'mun founds House of Wisdom.

1. Harun al-Rashid began his rule in _____ as part of the _____ dynasty.
2. Muhammad returned to Makkah in _____ .
3. The Battle of Tours took place in _____ . The _____ dynasty ruled at that time.
4. What event took place exactly a century before the Battle of Tours? _____
5. The *Hijrah* took place in _____ .
6. The Umayyad dynasty ended in _____ .
7. Muhammad experienced his first revelation in _____ .
8. The House of Wisdom was founded by _____ in _____ .
9. Ali was elected the fourth caliph in _____ .
10. Husayn was killed at the Battle of Karbala in _____ .

World History — Time Line Activities — 11

Name _____ Date _____ Class _____

Time Line Activity 12

The Rise Of Medieval Europe

By A.D. 1400, the seeds of what would become modern Europe had been planted. However, it took a number of events and shifts in power to reach that stage in development. The time line below plots some of the most important events in medieval European history. Read the time line, then answer the questions that follow.

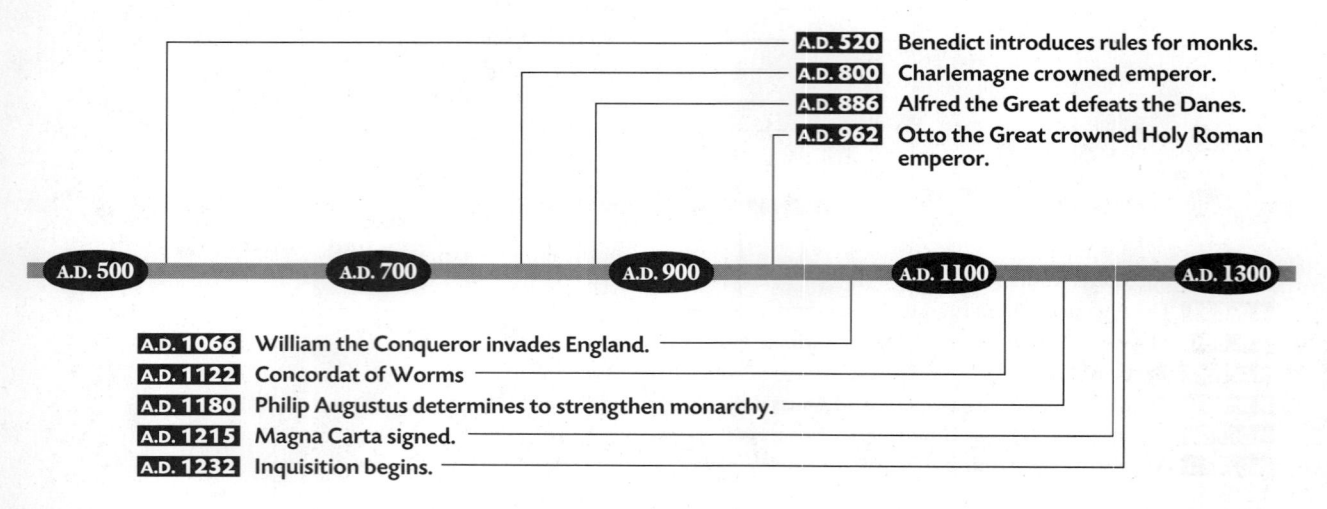

- **A.D. 520** Benedict introduces rules for monks.
- **A.D. 800** Charlemagne crowned emperor.
- **A.D. 886** Alfred the Great defeats the Danes.
- **A.D. 962** Otto the Great crowned Holy Roman emperor.

A.D. 500 — A.D. 700 — A.D. 900 — A.D. 1100 — A.D. 1300

- **A.D. 1066** William the Conqueror invades England.
- **A.D. 1122** Concordat of Worms
- **A.D. 1180** Philip Augustus determines to strengthen monarchy.
- **A.D. 1215** Magna Carta signed.
- **A.D. 1232** Inquisition begins.

1. Who began to rule the Holy Roman Empire in the A.D. 900s?
   _____

2. Who began to rule England in the A.D. 1000s?
   _____

3. In the early A.D. 1200s, King John of England had taken too much advantage of his royal powers. What was the result?
   _____

4. What was the result of the religious reform movement of the A.D. 1200s?
   _____

5. What event took place in the A.D. 1100s that led to Henry VII acquiring the power to name bishops?
   _____

6. Who was crowned the king of France in the late A.D. 1100s?
   _____

Name .... Date .... Class ....

Time Line Activity 13

Medieval Europe at Its Height

Medieval Europe in the years A.D. 1050–1500 underwent dramatic conflicts, innovation, and cultural diffusions. Some events of that time are shown on the time line below. Read the time line, then answer the questions that follow.

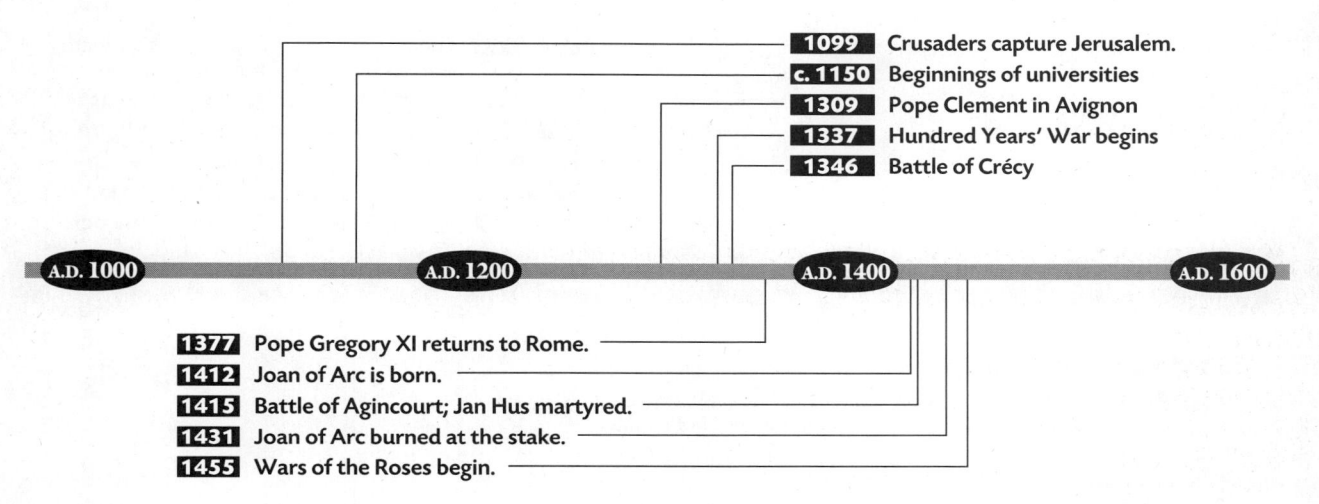

- **1099** Crusaders capture Jerusalem.
- **c. 1150** Beginnings of universities
- **1309** Pope Clement in Avignon
- **1337** Hundred Years' War begins
- **1346** Battle of Crécy

A.D. 1000 — A.D. 1200 — A.D. 1400 — A.D. 1600

- **1377** Pope Gregory XI returns to Rome.
- **1412** Joan of Arc is born.
- **1415** Battle of Agincourt; Jan Hus martyred.
- **1431** Joan of Arc burned at the stake.
- **1455** Wars of the Roses begin.

1. What important institutions began in the mid-twelfth century?

2. For how many years was the papal court out of Rome?

3. During which war was Joan of Arc alive?

4. How old was Joan of Arc when she died?

5. What were two important battles of the Hundred Years' War?

6. Who was the leader of the Czech reform movement burned at the stake in the first quarter of the fifteenth century?

7. What war between the English royal houses began in the 1400s?

Name _____ Date _____ Class _____

Time Line Activity 14

East and South Asia

In the centuries covered by Chapter 14, the civilizations of East and South Asia saw the rise and fall of many dynasties. Some political events are listed on the time line below. Read the time line, then answer the questions that follow.

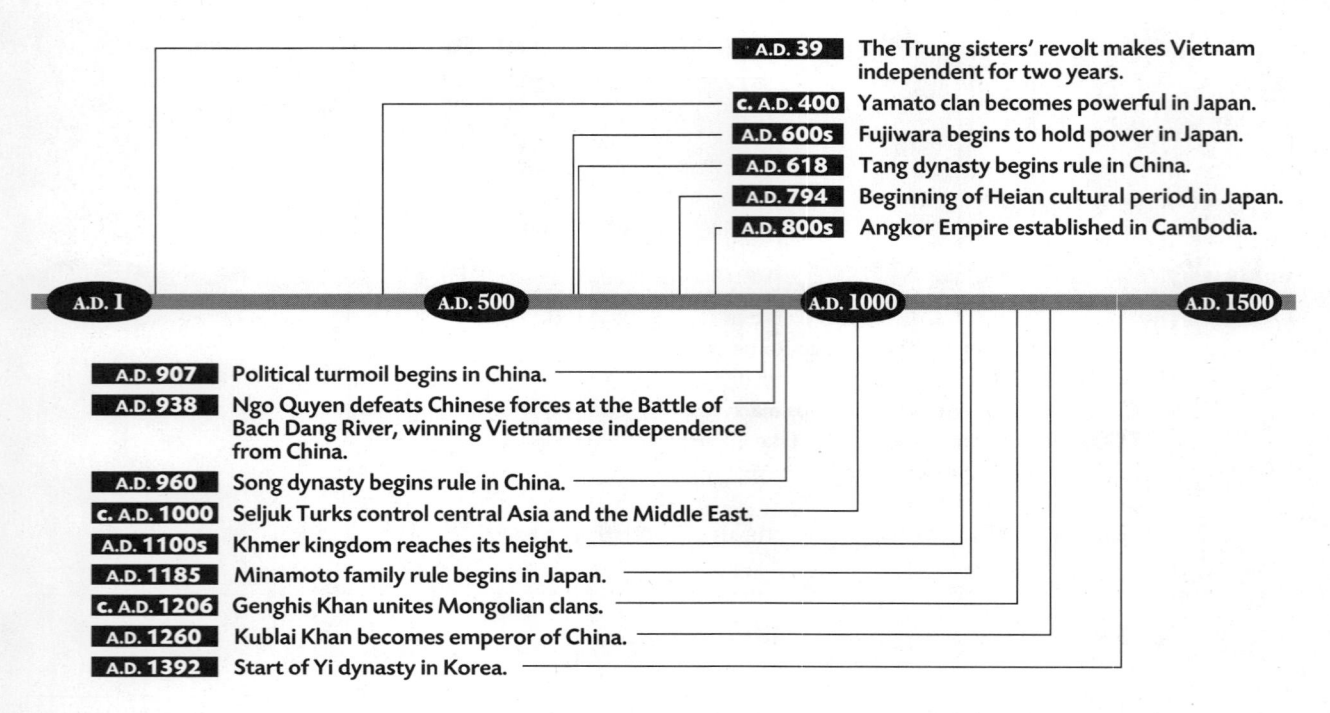

Above the line:
- A.D. 39 — The Trung sisters' revolt makes Vietnam independent for two years.
- c. A.D. 400 — Yamato clan becomes powerful in Japan.
- A.D. 600s — Fujiwara begins to hold power in Japan.
- A.D. 618 — Tang dynasty begins rule in China.
- A.D. 794 — Beginning of Heian cultural period in Japan.
- A.D. 800s — Angkor Empire established in Cambodia.

Time line markers: A.D. 1 — A.D. 500 — A.D. 1000 — A.D. 1500

Below the line:
- A.D. 907 — Political turmoil begins in China.
- A.D. 938 — Ngo Quyen defeats Chinese forces at the Battle of Bach Dang River, winning Vietnamese independence from China.
- A.D. 960 — Song dynasty begins rule in China.
- c. A.D. 1000 — Seljuk Turks control central Asia and the Middle East.
- A.D. 1100s — Khmer kingdom reaches its height.
- A.D. 1185 — Minamoto family rule begins in Japan.
- c. A.D. 1206 — Genghis Khan unites Mongolian clans.
- A.D. 1260 — Kublai Khan becomes emperor of China.
- A.D. 1392 — Start of Yi dynasty in Korea.

1. In the first half of the A.D. 900s, which Asian countries experienced political changes? _____

2. The Khmer kingdom established its empire in Angkor by A.D. 802 and ruled until 1431. When did this kingdom reach its highest achievements? _____

3. How did Genghis Khan's unification of Mongolia influence later events in China? _____

4. How long was Vietnam under Chinese rule? _____

5. Which kingdom was the last to establish a dynasty? What was the dynasty and when did it begin? _____

6. After political turmoil began in China in A.D. 907, would you say it was a short, moderate, or lengthy period before another Chinese dynasty was established? _____

Name .... Date .... Class ....

Time Line Activity 15

The Americas

Although information about many of the Mesoamerican civilizations remains sketchy, scholars continue to make discoveries about these peoples and the way they viewed the world. Read the time line below and answer the questions that follow.

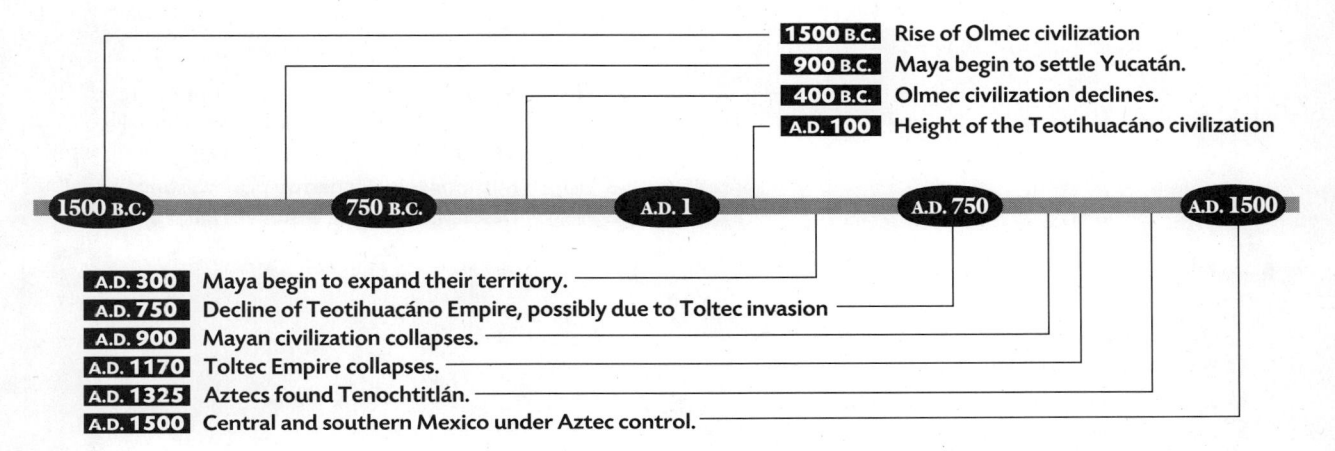

1500 B.C. Rise of Olmec civilization
900 B.C. Maya begin to settle Yucatán.
400 B.C. Olmec civilization declines.
A.D. 100 Height of the Teotihuacáno civilization

[Timeline: 1500 B.C. — 750 B.C. — A.D. 1 — A.D. 750 — A.D. 1500]

A.D. 300 Maya begin to expand their territory.
A.D. 750 Decline of Teotihuacáno Empire, possibly due to Toltec invasion
A.D. 900 Mayan civilization collapses.
A.D. 1170 Toltec Empire collapses.
A.D. 1325 Aztecs found Tenochtitlán.
A.D. 1500 Central and southern Mexico under Aztec control.

1. How many civilizations are charted on the time line?

2. Which other civilizations overlap in time with the Maya?

3. Why do you think these empires existed at the same time without conflict?

4. Some scholars have called the Olmec civilization the "mother culture" of Mexico. Explain why.

5. If you were an archaeologist and you discovered that a design found on an artifact at a Mayan site matched designs found at a Toltec site, what assumptions could you make and not make about that coincidence?

World History — Time Line Activities 15

Name .... Date .... Class ....

Time Line Activity 16

Renaissance and Reformation

The years A.D. 1350–1600 were a time of development and diffusion of cultural and political activity and a time of dissension and reform within religious institutions. New styles of art, learning, and commerce helped to generate important criticisms of the Catholic Church and, ultimately, the formation of Protestant religions. Read the time line below, then answer the questions that follow.

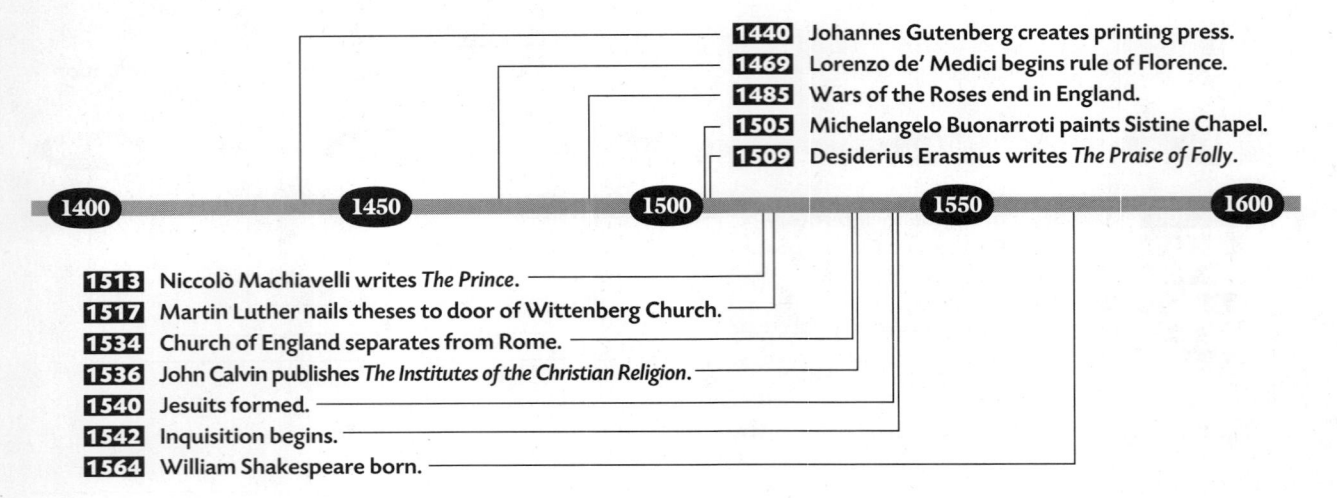

1440 Johannes Gutenberg creates printing press.
1469 Lorenzo de' Medici begins rule of Florence.
1485 Wars of the Roses end in England.
1505 Michelangelo Buonarroti paints Sistine Chapel.
1509 Desiderius Erasmus writes *The Praise of Folly*.

1400 — 1450 — 1500 — 1550 — 1600

1513 Niccolò Machiavelli writes *The Prince*.
1517 Martin Luther nails theses to door of Wittenberg Church.
1534 Church of England separates from Rome.
1536 John Calvin publishes *The Institutes of the Christian Religion*.
1540 Jesuits formed.
1542 Inquisition begins.
1564 William Shakespeare born.

1. Which event on the time line was most important for the diffusion of humanism?

2. What was the earliest critique of the practices of the Catholic Church?

3. Which critique of the practices of the Catholic Church led to the establishment of the first main Protestant religion?

4. What was the reason that humanism did not spread in England?

5. Which event on the time line helped curtail the spread of Protestantism and humanist books?

6. How many years elapsed after books were first printed before they were first banned?

7. Who wrote a book that influenced religious reformers for years to come?

Time Line Activity 17

Expanding Horizons

The explorations of the fifteenth and sixteenth centuries brought great changes to many civilizations. Read the time line below, then answer the questions that follow.

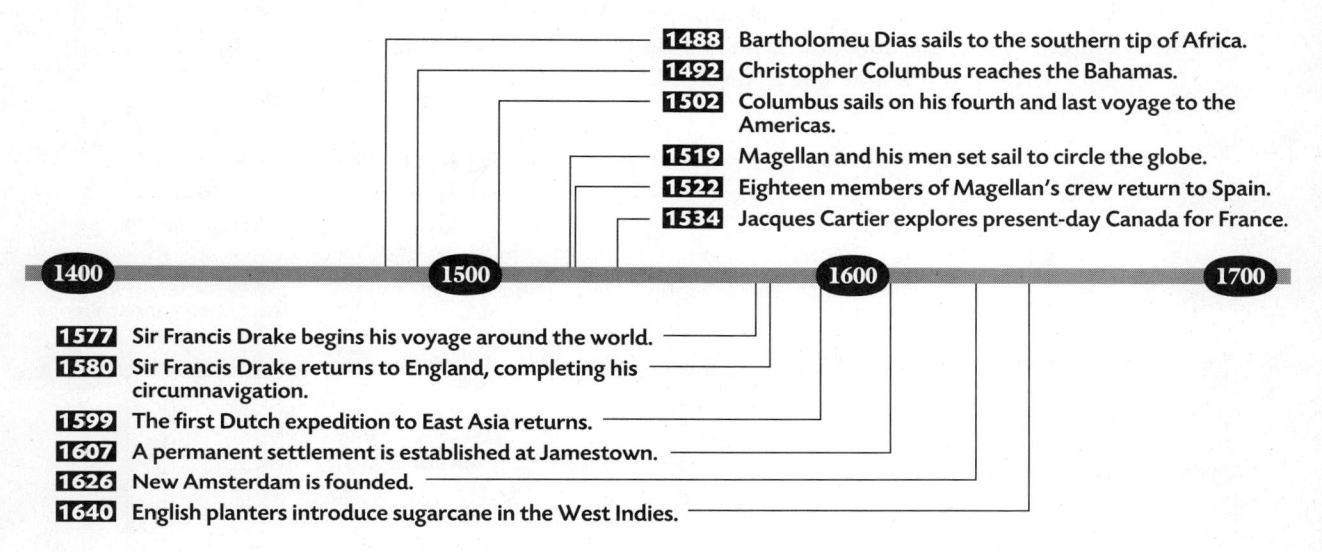

1488 Bartholomeu Dias sails to the southern tip of Africa.
1492 Christopher Columbus reaches the Bahamas.
1502 Columbus sails on his fourth and last voyage to the Americas.
1519 Magellan and his men set sail to circle the globe.
1522 Eighteen members of Magellan's crew return to Spain.
1534 Jacques Cartier explores present-day Canada for France.

1577 Sir Francis Drake begins his voyage around the world.
1580 Sir Francis Drake returns to England, completing his circumnavigation.
1599 The first Dutch expedition to East Asia returns.
1607 A permanent settlement is established at Jamestown.
1626 New Amsterdam is founded.
1640 English planters introduce sugarcane in the West Indies.

1. How long did it take Magellan's crew to circumnavigate the world?

2. How long did it take Sir Francis Drake to complete a similar trip?

3. How many years passed between Europeans first reaching the Americas and sugarcane being introduced in the West Indies?

4. When did Cartier explore present-day Canada for France?

5. Who first founded a settlement in the present-day United States: the English or the Dutch? What was it called?

Time Line Activity 18

Empires of Asia

The empires you have read about in Chapter 18 all faced both internal and external challenges to their stability and ways of life. From the Taiping Rebellion in China to the Young Ottomans' demands for reform, each attempt at change was met in a unique way by the empires involved. The time line below shows some changes that took place in Asian empires. Read the time line, then answer the questions that follow, adding information to the time line as directed.

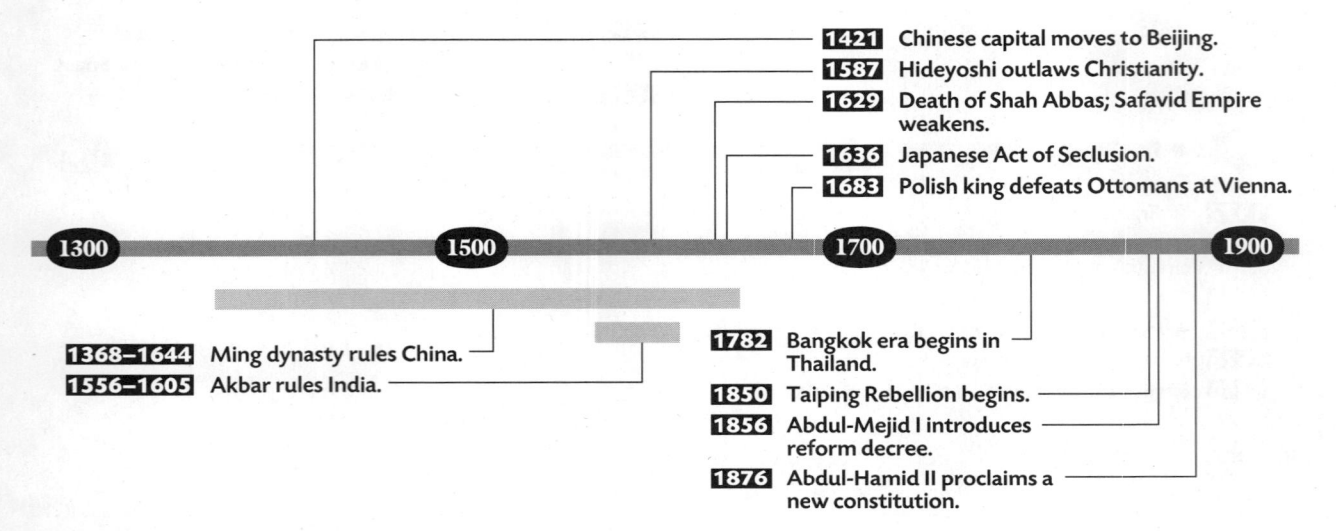

1421 Chinese capital moves to Beijing.
1587 Hideyoshi outlaws Christianity.
1629 Death of Shah Abbas; Safavid Empire weakens.
1636 Japanese Act of Seclusion.
1683 Polish king defeats Ottomans at Vienna.

1300 — 1500 — 1700 — 1900

1368–1644 Ming dynasty rules China.
1556–1605 Akbar rules India.
1782 Bangkok era begins in Thailand.
1850 Taiping Rebellion begins.
1856 Abdul-Mejid I introduces reform decree.
1876 Abdul-Hamid II proclaims a new constitution.

1. Who made the first attempts to reform the Ottoman Empire?

2. What two events happened in the Ottoman Empire in the year after Abdul-Hamid II proclaimed the new constitution? Add the events to the time line.

3. What event on the time line was the result of the conquest of Delhi at the Battle of Panipat?

4. What dynasty followed the Ming dynasty? Who started this dynasty? Add this information to the time line.

5. What event took place in Nagasaki after the Act of Seclusion? Add this information to the time line.

Name .... Date .... Class ....

Time Line Activity 19

Royal Power and Conflict

The monarchs who ruled Spain, England, France, the German states, and Russia from 1500 to 1750 were intent on expanding their territory and power. Their efforts at national expansion set the stage for Europe's future territorial conflicts. The time line below shows some of the key events in their power struggles. Read the time line, then answer the questions that follow.

1558 Elizabeth I becomes queen of England.
1567 Dutch Protestants rebel against Philip II's efforts to impose Catholicism on the Netherlands.
1587 Elizabeth I orders the execution of Mary Stuart, her cousin.
1588 England defeats the Spanish Armada.
1598 Russian Time of Troubles begins.
1618 Thirty Years' War begins.

1500 — 1600 — 1700 — 1800

1625 Huguenots revolt against Louis XIII.
1668 Spain recognizes Portugal's independence.
1685 The Edict of Nantes is repealed.
1700 Charles II dies; Europe is plunged into the War of the Spanish Succession.
1721 Russia defeats Sweden and wins control of the eastern end of the Baltic region.
1748 European powers sign the Treaty of Aix-la-Chapelle.

1. Whom did Queen Elizabeth I put to death in 1587? _____

2. When did the Thirty Years' War begin? _____

3. What common factor links the event that occurred in 1567 with the event in 1625?
_____
_____

4. Which country became independent in the mid-seventeenth century? _____

5. Based on the entire time line, how would you characterize Europe in the sixteenth, seventeenth, and early eighteenth centuries?
_____
_____
_____
_____

World History · Time Line Activities

Name _____ Date _____ Class _____

Time Line Activity 20

Scientific Revolution

During the scientific revolution, ideas changed the world. Look at the events listed on the time line. Write each event in the box next to the field of study it affected. Then describe the significance of the event. Events may be placed in more than one box.

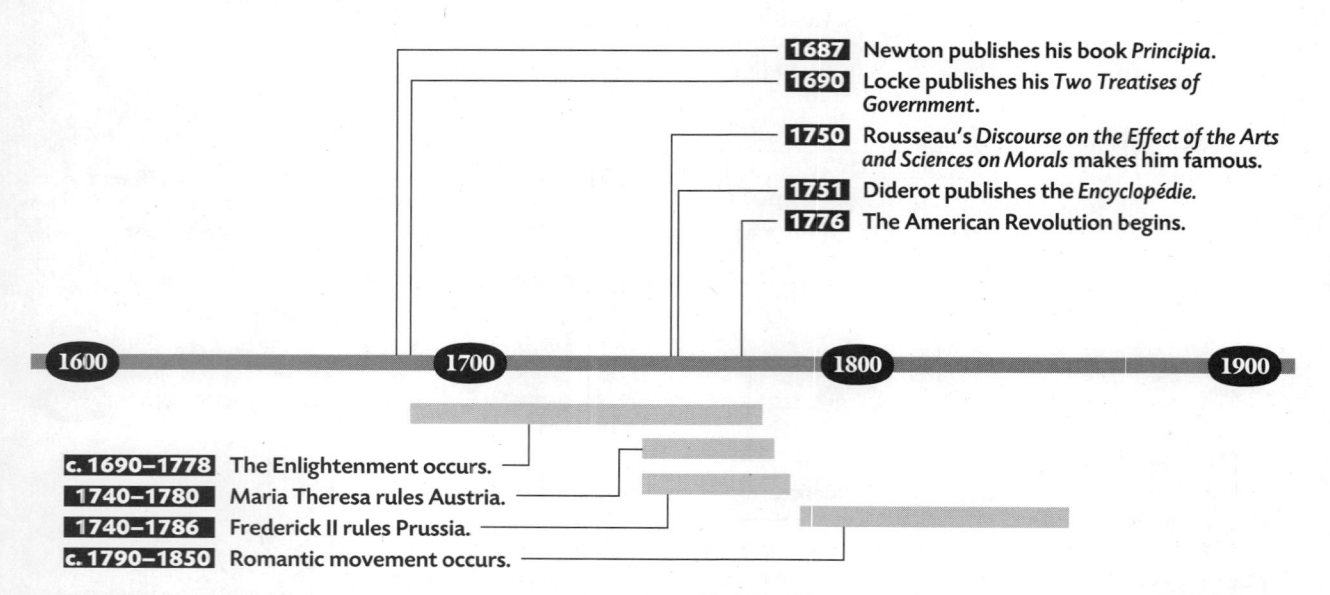

1687 Newton publishes his book *Principia*.
1690 Locke publishes his *Two Treatises of Government*.
1750 Rousseau's *Discourse on the Effect of the Arts and Sciences on Morals* makes him famous.
1751 Diderot publishes the *Encyclopédie*.
1776 The American Revolution begins.

1600 — 1700 — 1800 — 1900

c. 1690–1778 The Enlightenment occurs.
1740–1780 Maria Theresa rules Austria.
1740–1786 Frederick II rules Prussia.
c. 1790–1850 Romantic movement occurs.

Field	Event	Significance
Science/Mathematics		
Government/Politics		
Philosophy/Religion		
The Arts		

20 Time Line Activities World History

Name .... Date .... Class ....

Time Line Activity 21

English and American Revolutions

The 1600s and 1700s were a time of struggle for liberty in the English-speaking world. First in England, then in America, people fought against tyranny. The results of those struggles are still being felt today. Read the time line below, then answer the questions that follow.

1603 James I becomes king of England.
1625 Charles I becomes king of England.
1642 English Civil War begins.
1647 Charles I surrenders.
1649 Charles I is executed.
1653 Oliver Cromwell becomes lord protector.
1658 Cromwell dies.
1660 Charles II becomes king.
1688 Glorious Revolution
1689 English Bill of Rights

1600 — 1700 — 1800

1702 Queen Anne begins rule.
1714 George I beomes king.
1727 George II beomes king.
1760 George III beomes king.
1765 Stamp Act
1766 Stamp Act repealed
1770 Boston Massacre
1776 Declaration of Independence
1777 Battle of Saratoga
1781 Articles of Confederation
1787 Constitutional Convention

1. Which events occurred exactly a century apart? _____

2. How many years did the English Civil War last? _____

3. When did the Boston Massacre occur? _____

4. In what year did Oliver Cromwell become lord protector? _____

5. How long was the reign of James I? _____

6. Who was king during the American Revolution? _____

7. For how many years were the Articles of Confederation in effect? _____

8. What fact would lead you to conclude that colonial protests against the Stamp Act had an effect on the British Parliament?

_____

9. How many years before the U.S. Constitution was the Declaration of Independence written?

_____

World History — Time Line Activities **21**

Name .... Date .... Class ....

Time Line Activity 22

The French Revolution

In France, the years from 1789 to 1815 were turbulent. You can trace the changes that took place during this time in French history on a time line. Read the time line below. Then answer the questions that follow, adding information to the time line as directed.

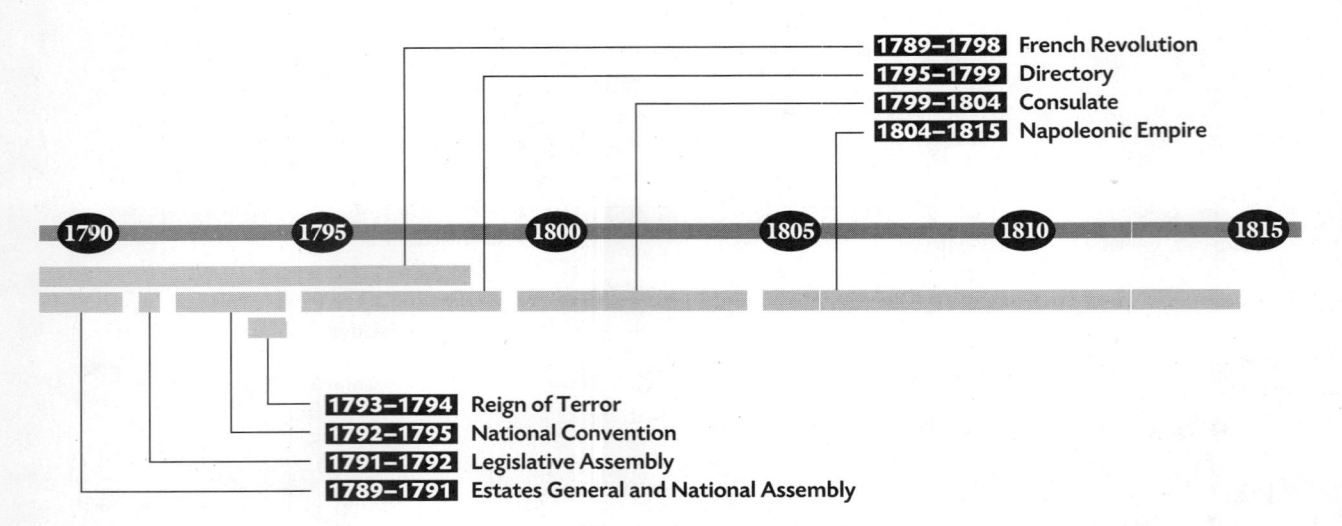

1789–1798 French Revolution
1795–1799 Directory
1799–1804 Consulate
1804–1815 Napoleonic Empire

[Timeline from 1790 to 1815]

1793–1794 Reign of Terror
1792–1795 National Convention
1791–1792 Legislative Assembly
1789–1791 Estates General and National Assembly

1. a. What event marked the beginning of the French Revolution? Add this point to the time line.

_____

b. How long did the French Revolution last? _____

2. a. What event marked the beginning of Napoleon's rule? Add this point to the time line.

_____

b. What event marked the end of Napoleon's rule? Add this point to the time line.

_____

3. Napoleon ruled from 1799 to 1815. The Consulate accounts for the years 1799 to 1804. The remaining years are called the Napoleonic Empire. What 1804 event caused the change? Write your answer below, then mark this point on your time line.

_____
_____

4. A French historian once said that the French Revolution "turned out badly." How does your time line illustrate this concept?

_____
_____

22   Time Line Activities   World History

Name .... Date .... Class ....

Time Line Activity 23

Age of Industry

The Industrial Revolution was a time of great change in England. An economy that had been based primarily on agriculture shifted to an economy based on manufacturing. Many people moved from small rural villages to cities and towns, and transportation of people and goods improved as roads and canals were built. The time line below shows some events of the Industrial Revolution. Read the time line and complete the activities that follow.

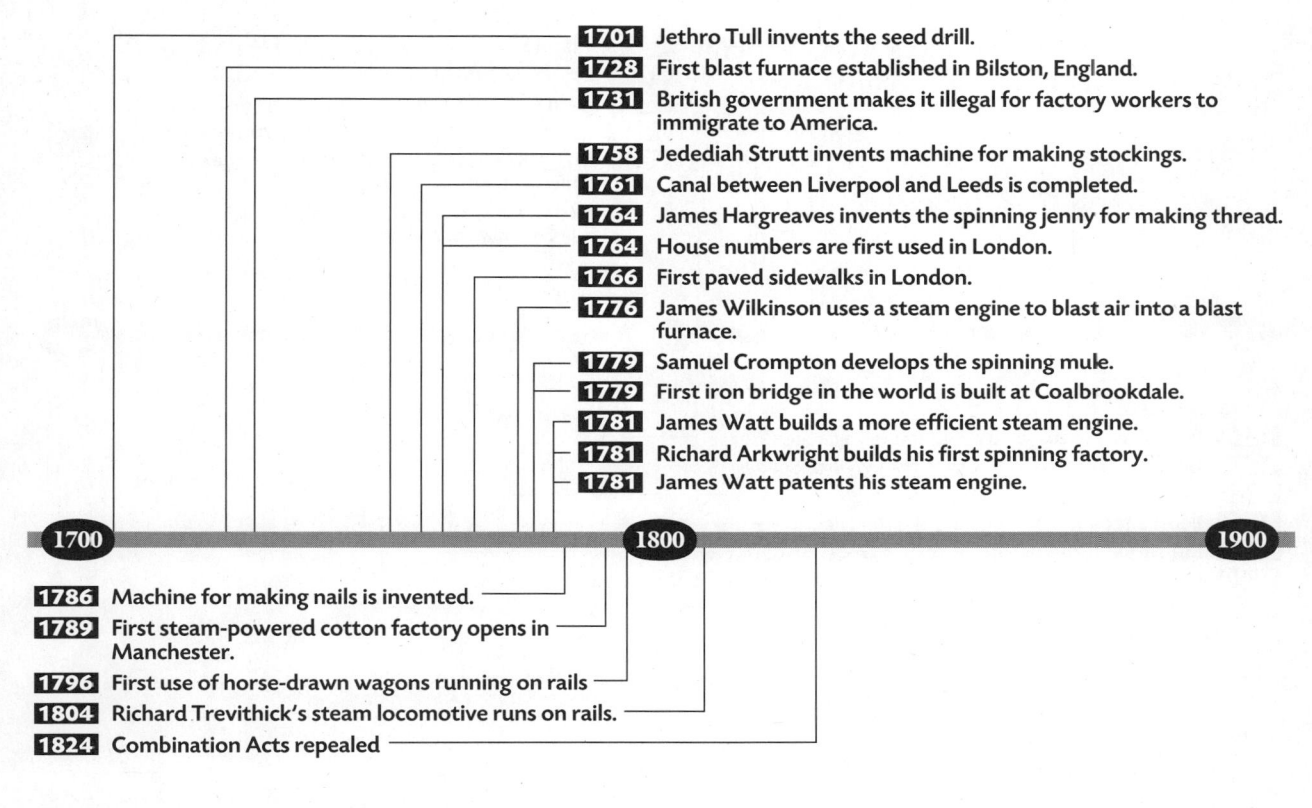

1701 Jethro Tull invents the seed drill.
1728 First blast furnace established in Bilston, England.
1731 British government makes it illegal for factory workers to immigrate to America.
1758 Jedediah Strutt invents machine for making stockings.
1761 Canal between Liverpool and Leeds is completed.
1764 James Hargreaves invents the spinning jenny for making thread.
1764 House numbers are first used in London.
1766 First paved sidewalks in London.
1776 James Wilkinson uses a steam engine to blast air into a blast furnace.
1779 Samuel Crompton develops the spinning mule.
1779 First iron bridge in the world is built at Coalbrookdale.
1781 James Watt builds a more efficient steam engine.
1781 Richard Arkwright builds his first spinning factory.
1781 James Watt patents his steam engine.

1700 ———————————— 1800 ———————————— 1900

1786 Machine for making nails is invented.
1789 First steam-powered cotton factory opens in Manchester.
1796 First use of horse-drawn wagons running on rails
1804 Richard Trevithick's steam locomotive runs on rails.
1824 Combination Acts repealed

1. What event on the time line is part of the agricultural revolution that preceded the Industrial Revolution? How did this invention improve farming?

2. What products mentioned in the time line were once produced under the domestic system?

3. What problem for weavers was the result of the invention of the spinning mule? What invention solved this problem? Add it to the time line.

4. What do the developments in London in 1764 and 1766 indicate about changes in cities?

World History   Time Line Activities   **23**

Name .... Date .... Class ....

Time Line Activity 24

Cultural Revolution

The period between 1750 and 1914 was a time of change in many areas. Changes in the way people thought about science, economics, and art laid the groundwork for the modern era. New developments in technology profoundly affected the way that people worked, traveled, and ate. Some changes even affected how many people there were and where they lived. Read the time line below, then answer the questions that follow.

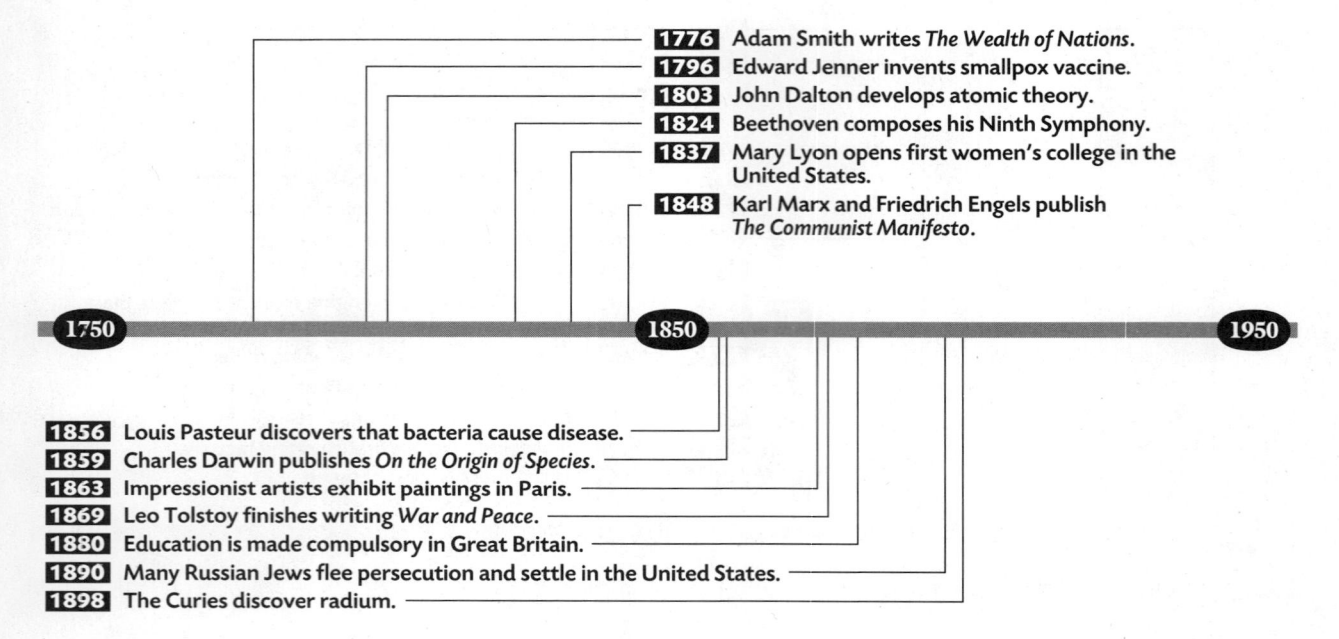

1776 Adam Smith writes *The Wealth of Nations*.
1796 Edward Jenner invents smallpox vaccine.
1803 John Dalton develops atomic theory.
1824 Beethoven composes his Ninth Symphony.
1837 Mary Lyon opens first women's college in the United States.
1848 Karl Marx and Friedrich Engels publish *The Communist Manifesto*.

1750 — 1850 — 1950

1856 Louis Pasteur discovers that bacteria cause disease.
1859 Charles Darwin publishes *On the Origin of Species*.
1863 Impressionist artists exhibit paintings in Paris.
1869 Leo Tolstoy finishes writing *War and Peace*.
1880 Education is made compulsory in Great Britain.
1890 Many Russian Jews flee persecution and settle in the United States.
1898 The Curies discover radium.

1. How many years passed between Jenner's invention of the smallpox vaccine and Pasteur's discovery that bacteria cause disease?

2. Scientists formulated the cell theory in 1838. What do atomic theory, cell theory, and the discovery of bacteria have in common?

3. How did these theories change the way people in Europe and North America viewed the world?

4. How many years passed between the writing of *The Wealth of Nations* and the writing of *The Communist Manifesto*?

5. Did the law making education compulsory in Great Britain reflect the philosophy of *The Wealth of Nations*, *The Communist Manifesto*, or some other influence? Explain.

24   Time Line Activities   World History

Name .... Date .... Class ....

Time Line Activity 25

Democracy and Reform

During the 1800s and early 1900s, countries struggled for independence, rights, and lands. Some events of this period are shown on the time line below. Use the time line to answer the questions that follow.

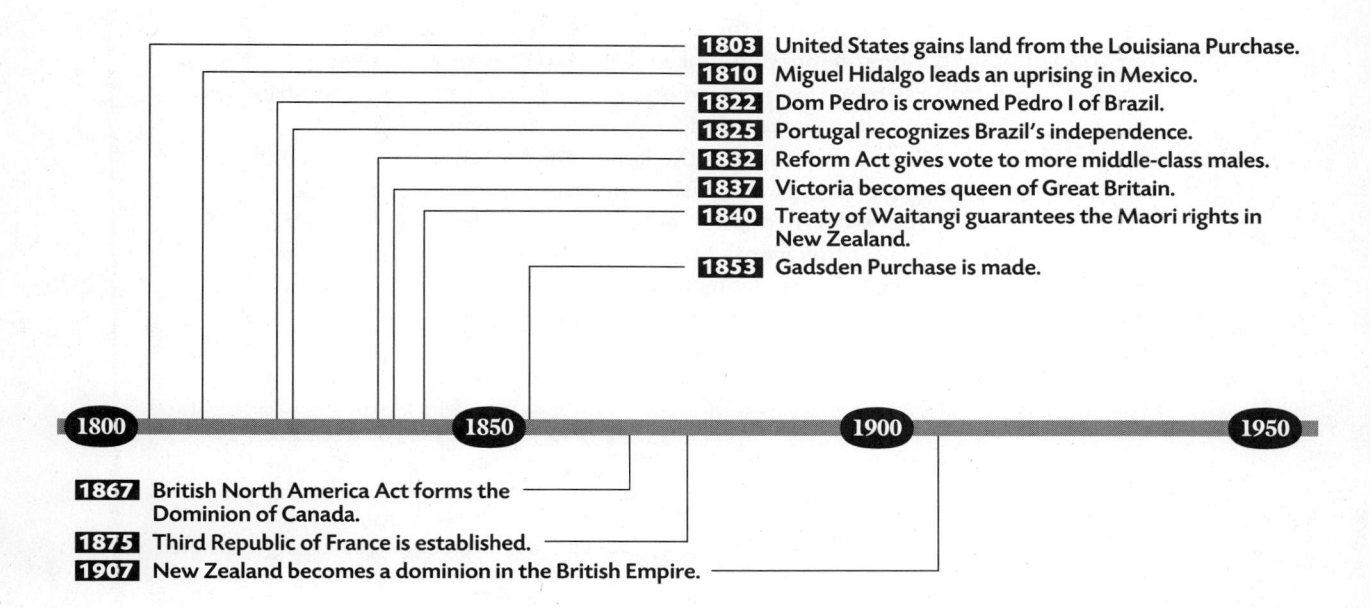

1803 United States gains land from the Louisiana Purchase.
1810 Miguel Hidalgo leads an uprising in Mexico.
1822 Dom Pedro is crowned Pedro I of Brazil.
1825 Portugal recognizes Brazil's independence.
1832 Reform Act gives vote to more middle-class males.
1837 Victoria becomes queen of Great Britain.
1840 Treaty of Waitangi guarantees the Maori rights in New Zealand.
1853 Gadsden Purchase is made.

1800 — 1850 — 1900 — 1950

1867 British North America Act forms the Dominion of Canada.
1875 Third Republic of France is established.
1907 New Zealand becomes a dominion in the British Empire.

1. Which was passed first, the Reform Act or the British North America Act?
   _____

2. How long after Dom Pedro was crowned emperor did Portugal recognize Brazil's independence?
   _____

3. How long after the Louisiana Purchase was the Gadsden Purchase made?
   _____

4. Which occurred later, Queen Victoria's coronation or the signing of the Treaty of Waitangi?
   _____

5. How long after the signing of the Treaty of Waitangi did New Zealand become a dominion?
   _____

World History   Time Line Activities   **25**

Time Line Activity 26

Reaction and Nationalism

Can an idea be more powerful than a king or an emperor? Nationalism is an idea that has driven out kings and toppled empires. Between 1815 and 1914, nationalism changed the map of Europe. Two countries—Italy and Germany—emerged from collections of independent states. The empire of Austria-Hungary came apart as the idea of nationalism inspired people to demand independence. In related movements, people throughout Europe demanded freedom of the press, freedom of speech, freedom to elect representatives, and relief from feudal systems of labor and taxes. Of course, none of the rulers of the kingdoms and empires threatened by these movements gave up power easily. The forces of nationalism and reform were often met with reactions opposing their progress. Read the time line below. Then decide if the events on the line express the success of movements demanding change or reactions to those movements. List events in the appropriate column of the chart below. Some items may be included in both columns.

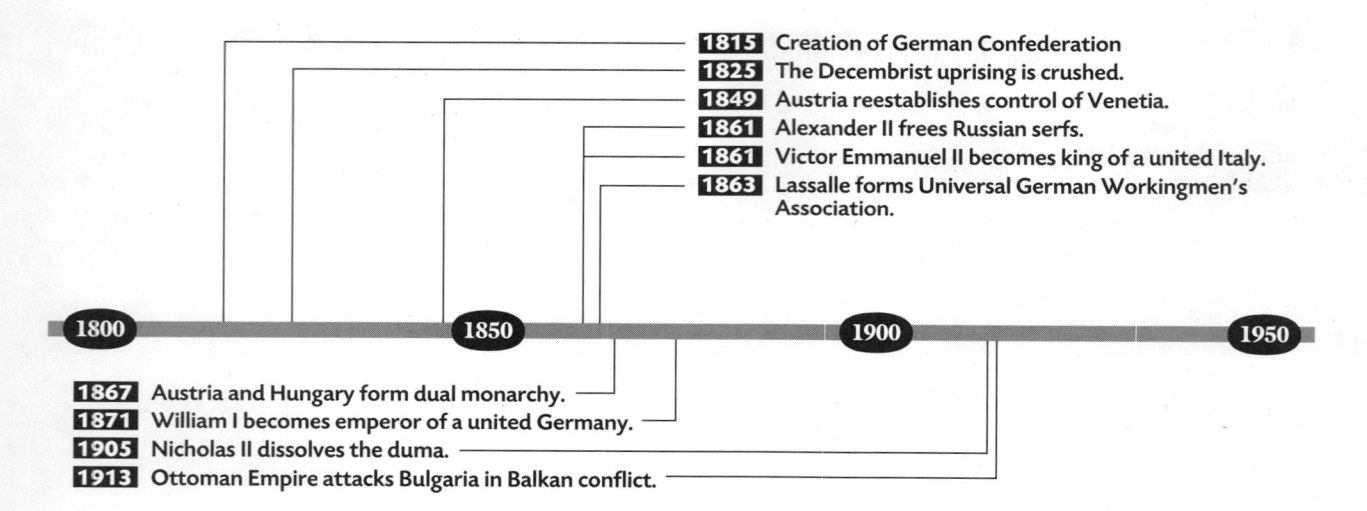

1815 Creation of German Confederation
1825 The Decembrist uprising is crushed.
1849 Austria reestablishes control of Venetia.
1861 Alexander II frees Russian serfs.
1861 Victor Emmanuel II becomes king of a united Italy.
1863 Lassalle forms Universal German Workingmen's Association.

1800 — 1850 — 1900 — 1950

1867 Austria and Hungary form dual monarchy.
1871 William I becomes emperor of a united Germany.
1905 Nicholas II dissolves the duma.
1913 Ottoman Empire attacks Bulgaria in Balkan conflict.

Nationalism/Reform	Reaction

Name .... Date .... Class ....

Time Line Activity 27

The Age of Imperialism

Nineteenth-century social, political, and economic factors led to a period of expansion called the Age of Imperialism. During this period, European countries divided Africa, India, and China among themselves, while the United States extended its power into Latin America. The time line below lists some of the key events in this period of expansion. Study the events shown on the time line. Then complete the chart by selecting any five events from the time line and explaining how they were examples of imperialism. First, check off which factors the event most strongly influenced: social, political, or economic. Then write a sentence justifying your choice. One event has been completed for you as a model.

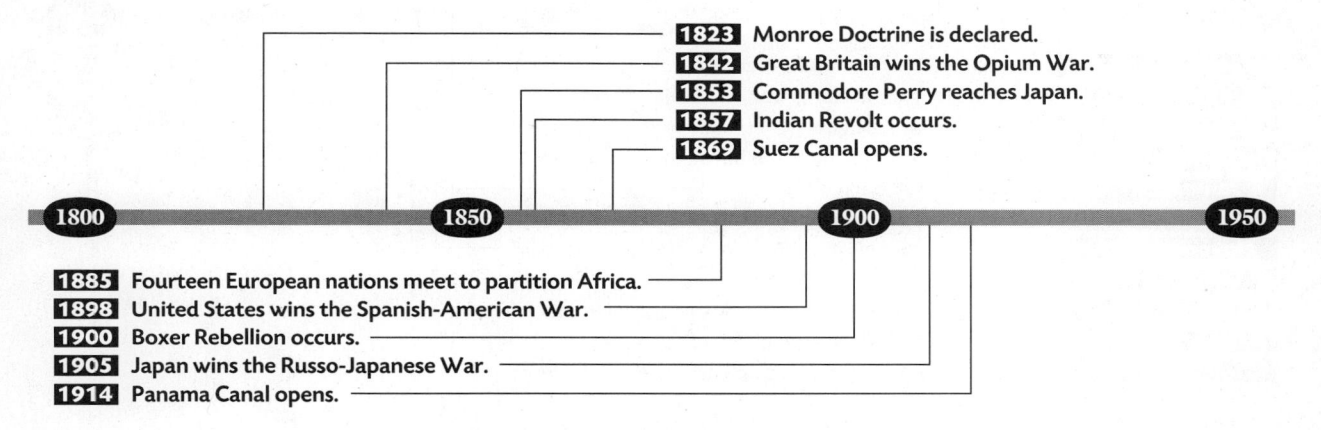

1823 Monroe Doctrine is declared.
1842 Great Britain wins the Opium War.
1853 Commodore Perry reaches Japan.
1857 Indian Revolt occurs.
1869 Suez Canal opens.

1800 — 1850 — 1900 — 1950

1885 Fourteen European nations meet to partition Africa.
1898 United States wins the Spanish-American War.
1900 Boxer Rebellion occurs.
1905 Japan wins the Russo-Japanese War.
1914 Panama Canal opens.

IMPERIALISM

Event	Social	Political	Economic	Explanation
Monroe Doctrine is declared.		X		Extended American interests in Latin America.

World History — Time Line Activities

Name _____ Date _____ Class _____

Time Line Activity 28

World War I

Look at the events listed on the time line. Write each event in the chart below next to the theme it represents, caused, or resulted from. In the right-hand column, explain how each event is related to the theme. Try to place events in more than one category.

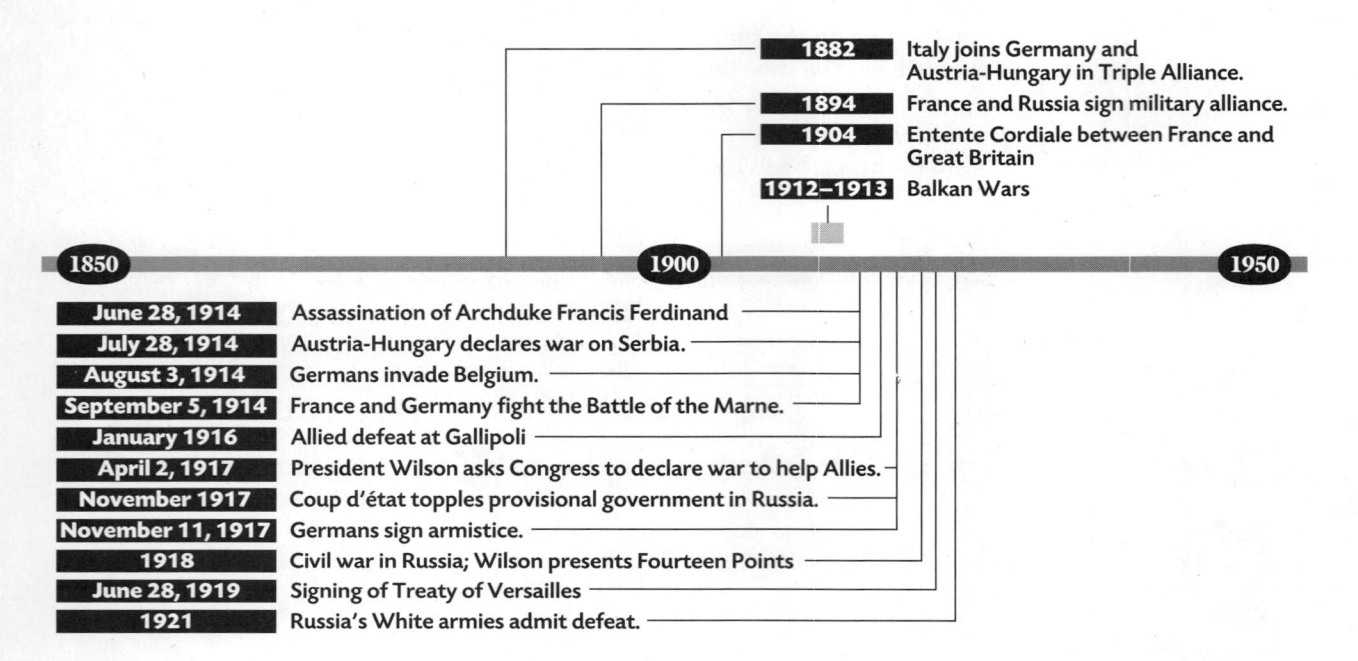

1882 Italy joins Germany and Austria-Hungary in Triple Alliance.
1894 France and Russia sign military alliance.
1904 Entente Cordiale between France and Great Britain
1912–1913 Balkan Wars

1850 — 1900 — 1950

June 28, 1914 Assassination of Archduke Francis Ferdinand
July 28, 1914 Austria-Hungary declares war on Serbia.
August 3, 1914 Germans invade Belgium.
September 5, 1914 France and Germany fight the Battle of the Marne.
January 1916 Allied defeat at Gallipoli
April 2, 1917 President Wilson asks Congress to declare war to help Allies.
November 1917 Coup d'état topples provisional government in Russia.
November 11, 1917 Germans sign armistice.
1918 Civil war in Russia; Wilson presents Fourteen Points
June 28, 1919 Signing of Treaty of Versailles
1921 Russia's White armies admit defeat.

Theme	Event	Explanation
Cooperation	Italy joins Germany and Austria-Hungary in Triple Alliance.	Alliance brings countries together to support one another against aggressors.
Conflict	Signing of Treaty of Versailles	
Revolution		
Internationalism		

28   Time Line Activities   World History

Name _____ Date _____ Class _____

Time Line Activity 29

Between Two Fires

Many changes took place in Europe and the United States in the years after World War I. Some of these events are listed on the time line below. Read the time line, then answer the questions that follow.

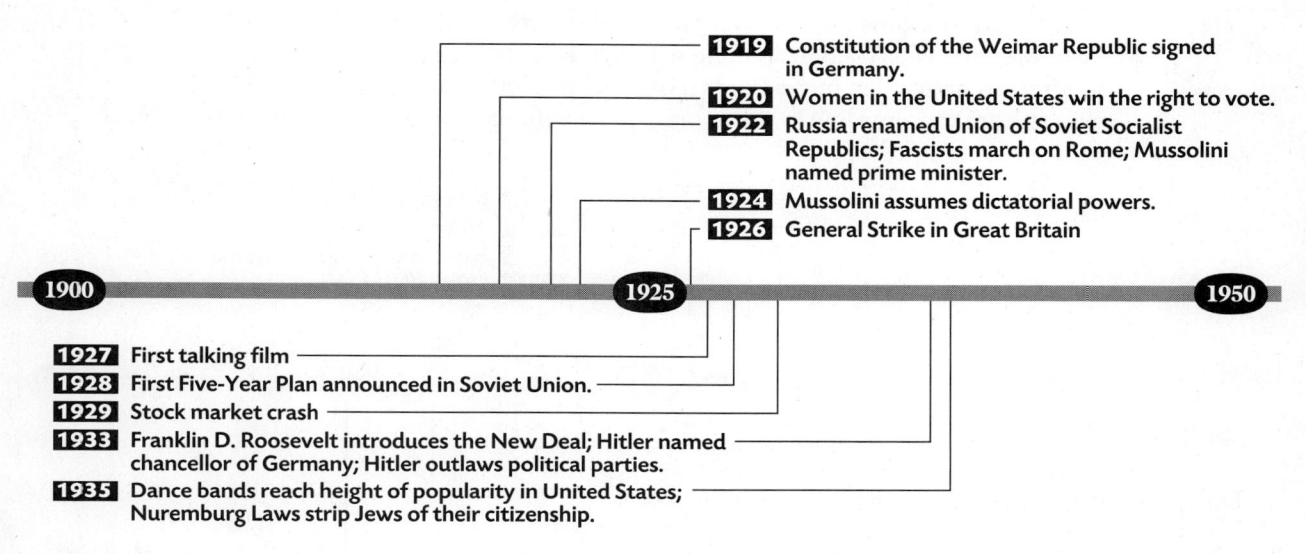

1919 Constitution of the Weimar Republic signed in Germany.
1920 Women in the United States win the right to vote.
1922 Russia renamed Union of Soviet Socialist Republics; Fascists march on Rome; Mussolini named prime minister.
1924 Mussolini assumes dictatorial powers.
1926 General Strike in Great Britain

1900 —————————— 1925 —————————— 1950

1927 First talking film
1928 First Five-Year Plan announced in Soviet Union.
1929 Stock market crash
1933 Franklin D. Roosevelt introduces the New Deal; Hitler named chancellor of Germany; Hitler outlaws political parties.
1935 Dance bands reach height of popularity in United States; Nuremburg Laws strip Jews of their citizenship.

1. After which year could American women participate in choosing the President?
   _____

2. How long did the Weimar Republic last? _____

3. Jewish people had no rights in Germany after which year? _____

4. a. In which western European country did a totalitarian leader first take control?
   _____

   b. Who was the leader? _____

5. a. What economic disaster happened in the 1920s? _____

   b. In which year did this happen? _____

6. In which year did the Communists finally assume total control in Russia?
   _____

7. When did the first Five-Year Plan end in the Soviet Union? _____

World History   Time Line Activities   29

Name _____ Date _____ Class _____

Time Line Activity 30

Nationalism in Asia, Africa, and Latin America

Hope for a new world after World War I led people in China, India, the Middle East, and Africa to embrace the cause of nationalism. In Japan, a nationalist spirit led to militarism and expansionism. Nationalists in several countries of Latin America resisted U.S. intervention in that region. The time line below lists several events of this period in history. Read the time line. Then determine whether each of the events resulted from or affected nationalist movements in Asia, Africa, or Latin America. List the events from the time line in the appropriate columns on the chart below.

1917 Balfour Declaration
1919 Amritsar Massacre
1921 Harry Thuku organizes nationalists.
1925 Chiang Kai-shek sets up government at Nanjing.

1900 —————— 1925 —————— 1950

1930 Prime Minister Osachi Hamaguchi assassinated; Mohandas K. Gandhi leads salt tax march.
1933 Franklin D. Roosevelt announces Good Neighbor policy.
1934 Mao Zedong leads the Long March.
1937 President Getúlio Vargas proclaims a new constitution; Nnamdi Azikwe starts a newspaper.
1938 Lázaro Cárdenas nationalizes oil wells.

Location	Event
Asia	
Africa	
Latin America	

30   Time Line Activities   World History

Name _____ Date _____ Class _____

Time Line Activity 31

World War II

After World War I, territorial aggression and minor conflicts during the 1930s laid the groundwork for another major war. Tensions among European nations had become so strong by 1939 that it took only a spark—Germany's invasion of Poland—to ignite World War II. Read the time line. Then, for each outcome listed below, write the year and event that led to that outcome.

1931 Japan invades Chinese province of Manchuria.
1935 Italy invades Ethiopia.
1936 Spanish Civil War begins; Germany occupies Rhineland.
1937 Japan attacks China.
1938 *Anschluss* plan to group all German peoples into one country is put into action; Munich Conference
1939 Spanish Civil War ends; Nazi-Soviet Nonaggression Pact; Germany invades Poland; World War II begins.

1930 — 1940 — 1950

1940 Germans enter Paris and France surrenders; Germany begins blitz of London.
1941 Germany invades Soviet Union; Japan attacks U.S. naval base at Pearl Harbor.
1943 Allies invade island of Sicily.
1944 D-Day: Allies invade Normandy.
1945 Germany surrenders; United States drops atomic bombs on Hiroshima and Nagasaki.

1. Nation is divided; Germans occupy the capital and the northern half while collaborationist government is set up in southern part in the city of Vichy.

   Year _____ Event _____

2. Complete devastation of cities forces Japan to surrender.

   Year _____ Event _____

3. Germany and Italy aid the Nationalist forces led by Franco against the opposing Loyalist forces.

   Year _____ Event _____

4. Foreign aggression in the Pacific brings the United States into the war.

   Year _____ Event _____

5. Germany occupies and annexes Austria.

   Year _____ Event _____

6. Counterattack launched to roll back Axis forces from Italian peninsula.

   Year _____ Event _____

World History   Time Line Activities   **31**

Name _____ Date _____ Class _____

Time Line Activity 32

The Cold War

Recovery from destruction caused by World War II required a level of international cooperation never before attempted. Ironically, at the same time a new global conflict—the cold war—brought the world to a new level of danger. Review the time line below. Write each date and event from the time line in the chart, classifying each event as a conflict or a cooperative effort (or both, if applicable).

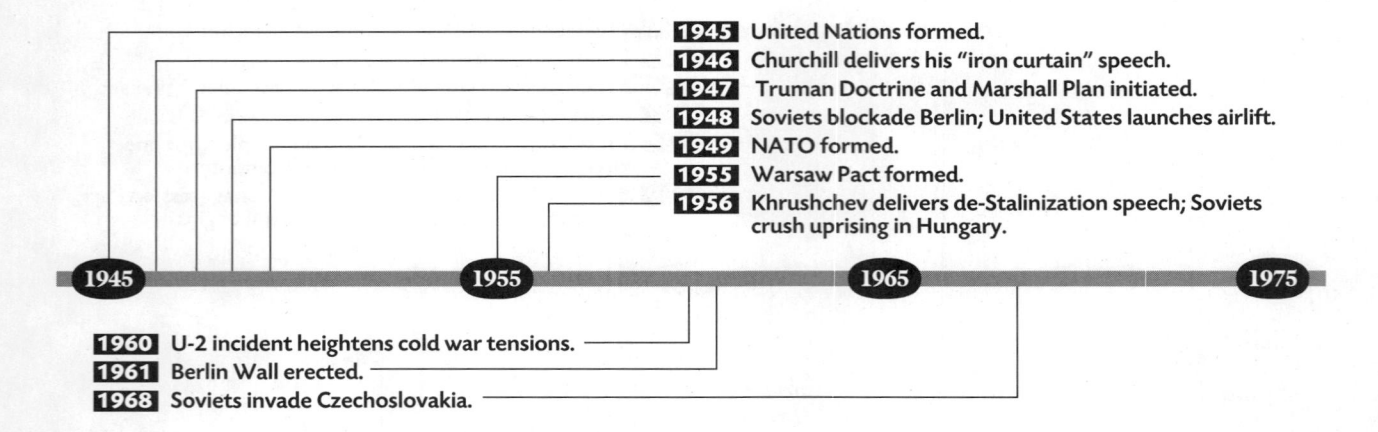

1945 United Nations formed.
1946 Churchill delivers his "iron curtain" speech.
1947 Truman Doctrine and Marshall Plan initiated.
1948 Soviets blockade Berlin; United States launches airlift.
1949 NATO formed.
1955 Warsaw Pact formed.
1956 Khrushchev delivers de-Stalinization speech; Soviets crush uprising in Hungary.

1945 — 1955 — 1965 — 1975

1960 U-2 incident heightens cold war tensions.
1961 Berlin Wall erected.
1968 Soviets invade Czechoslovakia.

Date	Conflict	Cooperative Effort

Time Line Activities — World History

Name _____ Date _____ Class _____

Time Line Activity 33

Asia and the Pacific

The years since World War II have been a time of great change and growth in Asia and the Pacific region. Many countries have emerged as world economic powers, and China and India, the two most populous nations in the world, continue to grow in influence. Read the time line below and answer the questions that follow.

1945 World War II ends
1947 India and Pakistan become independent.
1948 Mohandas Gandhi is assassinated.
1949 Communists take power in China.
1950 Korean War begins.
1951 ANZUS treaty is signed.
1953 Korean War ends.
1954 Battle of Dien Bien Phu
1958 Great Leap Forward begins.
1964 Tonkin Gulf Resolution

1940 — 1965 — 1990

1965 Ferdinand Marcos is elected Philippine president.
1971 Civil war in Pakistan
1972 President Nixon goes to China.
1973 United States leaves Vietnam.
1984 Indira Gandhi is assassinated.
1985 New Zealand bars ships carrying nuclear weapons from its waters.
1986 Corazon Aquino replaces Marcos in Philippines.

1. In what year did the Korean War begin? _____

2. How many years separated the assassinations of Indira Ghandi and Mohandas Gandhi? _____

3. Pakistan's civil war occurred how many years after its independence? _____

4. For how many years did Ferdinand Marcos rule the Philippines? _____

5. U.S. assistance to Vietnam began after the Battle of Dien Bien Phu. For how many years was the United States involved in Vietnam? _____

6. How many years after the end of World War II did the Communists take power in China? _____

7. In what year did President Nixon visit China? _____

8. How many years following the signing of the ANZUS treaty did New Zealand bar ships carrying nuclear weapons from its waters? _____

9. In what year was the Tonkin Gulf Resolution passed? _____

10. The Great Leap Forward was ended in 1960. For how many years did it last?

World History — Time Line Activities — **33**

Name _____ Date _____ Class _____

Time Line Activity 34

Africa

The years after World War II were times of great change in Africa. Colonies became independent nations, some of which were split by civil wars. Leaders rose to power and were replaced. The time line below shows some of the events that took place in Africa. Read the time line, then answer the questions that follow.

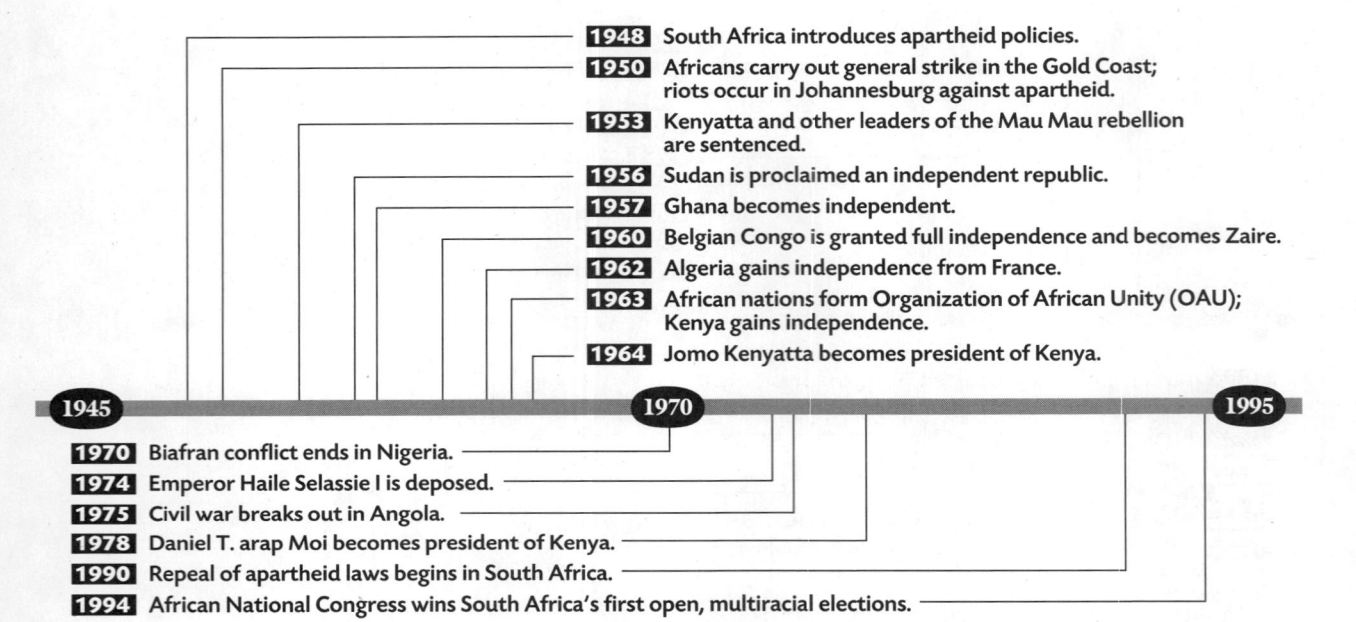

1948 South Africa introduces apartheid policies.
1950 Africans carry out general strike in the Gold Coast; riots occur in Johannesburg against apartheid.
1953 Kenyatta and other leaders of the Mau Mau rebellion are sentenced.
1956 Sudan is proclaimed an independent republic.
1957 Ghana becomes independent.
1960 Belgian Congo is granted full independence and becomes Zaire.
1962 Algeria gains independence from France.
1963 African nations form Organization of African Unity (OAU); Kenya gains independence.
1964 Jomo Kenyatta becomes president of Kenya.

1945 — 1970 — 1995

1970 Biafran conflict ends in Nigeria.
1974 Emperor Haile Selassie I is deposed.
1975 Civil war breaks out in Angola.
1978 Daniel T. arap Moi becomes president of Kenya.
1990 Repeal of apartheid laws begins in South Africa.
1994 African National Congress wins South Africa's first open, multiracial elections.

1. Which African nation first gained its independence: Belgian Congo, Kenya, Algeria, or Sudan?

2. When did the nation of Zaire gain its independence?

3. How much time passed from Jomo Kenyatta's imprisonment to his election as the first president of independent Kenya?

4. Which covered a shorter amount of time: the period of apartheid in South Africa or Jomo Kenyatta's presidency?

5. Which was longer: the period from the introduction of apartheid to the first race riots, or the period from the repeal of apartheid to open, multiracial elections in South Africa?

34 Time Line Activities World History

Name .... Date .... Class ....

Time Line Activity 35

The Middle East

Bringing peace to the Middle East is an ongoing struggle that has involved many nations, both inside as well as outside the region. Unresolved conflicts over religion, territory, resources, and the balance of political power have led to wars and terrorism. At the same time, real progress has been made within the region. The time line below shows the conflicts and attempts at finding peace. Read the time line, then answer the questions that follow.

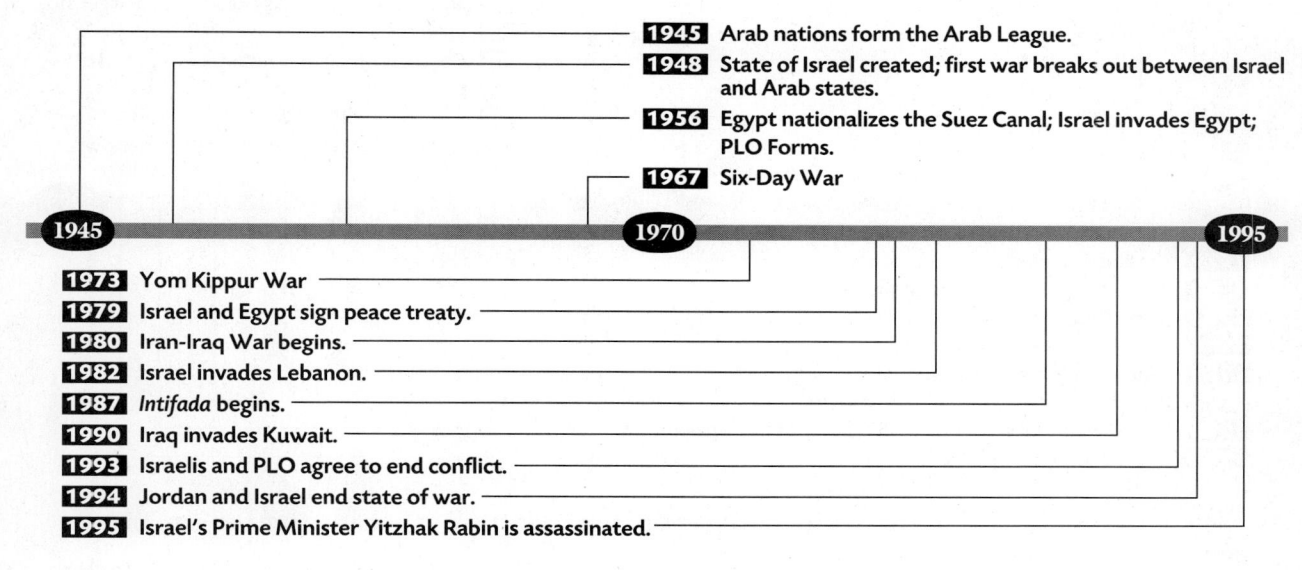

1945 Arab nations form the Arab League.
1948 State of Israel created; first war breaks out between Israel and Arab states.
1956 Egypt nationalizes the Suez Canal; Israel invades Egypt; PLO Forms.
1967 Six-Day War

1945 —————————————— 1970 —————————————— 1995

1973 Yom Kippur War
1979 Israel and Egypt sign peace treaty.
1980 Iran-Iraq War begins.
1982 Israel invades Lebanon.
1987 *Intifada* begins.
1990 Iraq invades Kuwait.
1993 Israelis and PLO agree to end conflict.
1994 Jordan and Israel end state of war.
1995 Israel's Prime Minister Yitzhak Rabin is assassinated.

1. How many of the events shown on the time line led to increased conflict?
_____

2. How many of the events shown on the time line represent steps taken toward peace?
_____

3. In the space below, make two time lines of your own, using the events shown or events described in your textbook. The first time line will show conflicts in the Middle East. The second will show steps toward peace. What do you notice about your time lines?
_____

Conflict

1945 —————————————— 1970 —————————————— 1995

Peace

1945 —————————————— 1970 —————————————— 1995

World History — Time Line Activities — 35

Time Line Activity 36

Latin America

The last 50 years have brought many changes to the people and countries of Latin America. Violence in the form of civil wars and revolution, economic growth despite continued poverty, and, in recent years, a turn toward democracy have combined to make the post–World War II era a turning point in the region's history. Look at the time line below and answer the questions that follow.

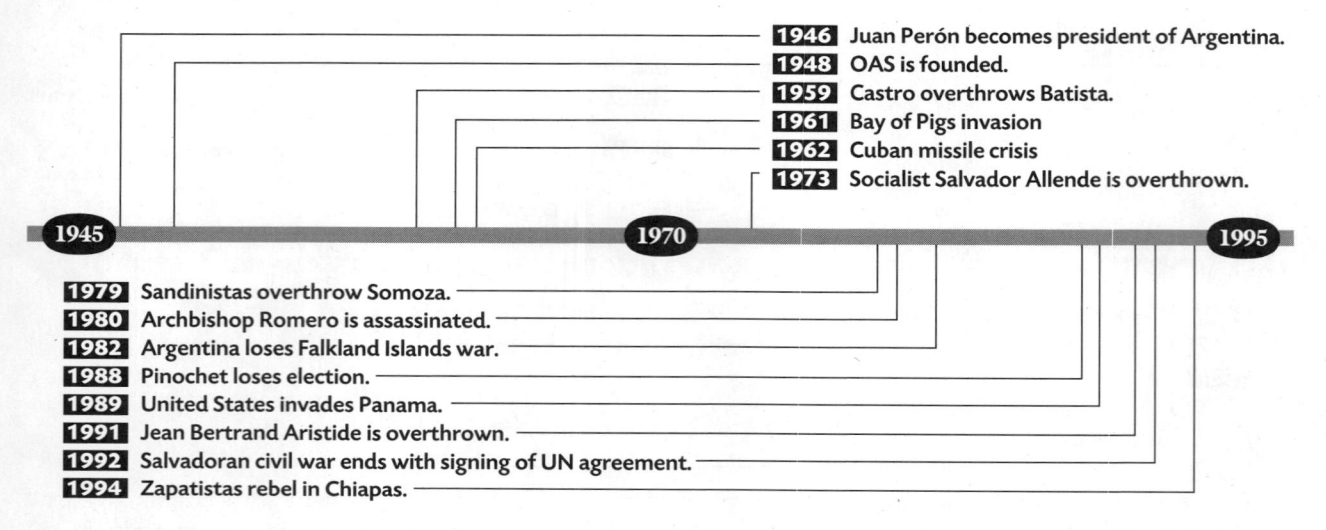

1946 Juan Perón becomes president of Argentina.
1948 OAS is founded.
1959 Castro overthrows Batista.
1961 Bay of Pigs invasion
1962 Cuban missile crisis
1973 Socialist Salvador Allende is overthrown.

1945 — 1970 — 1995

1979 Sandinistas overthrow Somoza.
1980 Archbishop Romero is assassinated.
1982 Argentina loses Falkland Islands war.
1988 Pinochet loses election.
1989 United States invades Panama.
1991 Jean Bertrand Aristide is overthrown.
1992 Salvadoran civil war ends with signing of UN agreement.
1994 Zapatistas rebel in Chiapas.

1. What four people were overthrown as leaders of their countries? In what years and in which countries were these leaders forced from power?

2. How many years after Castro came to power was his country involved in a severe cold war crisis with the United States? What was the crisis called?

3. For how many years did the leader who replaced Salvador Allende rule his country? What was this leader's name?

4. Three years after the United States invaded Panama, its leader was convicted of drug-trafficking charges. What was the date and who was the leader? Add this information to the time line.

5. Following the murder of a popular religious figure, a civil war erupted in this country. What is the country? How long did the civil war last?

6. Eleven years after Nicaragua's longtime dictator was overthrown, a woman was elected president in free, democratic elections. What was the date and who was the woman? Add this information to the time line.

36 Time Line Activities World History

Name .... Date .... Class ....

Time Line Activity 37

The World in Transition

North America and Europe have seen tremendous changes in the last few decades. Some events of this period are shown on the time line below. Read the time line. Then use the information from the time line and your textbook to complete the chart that follows.

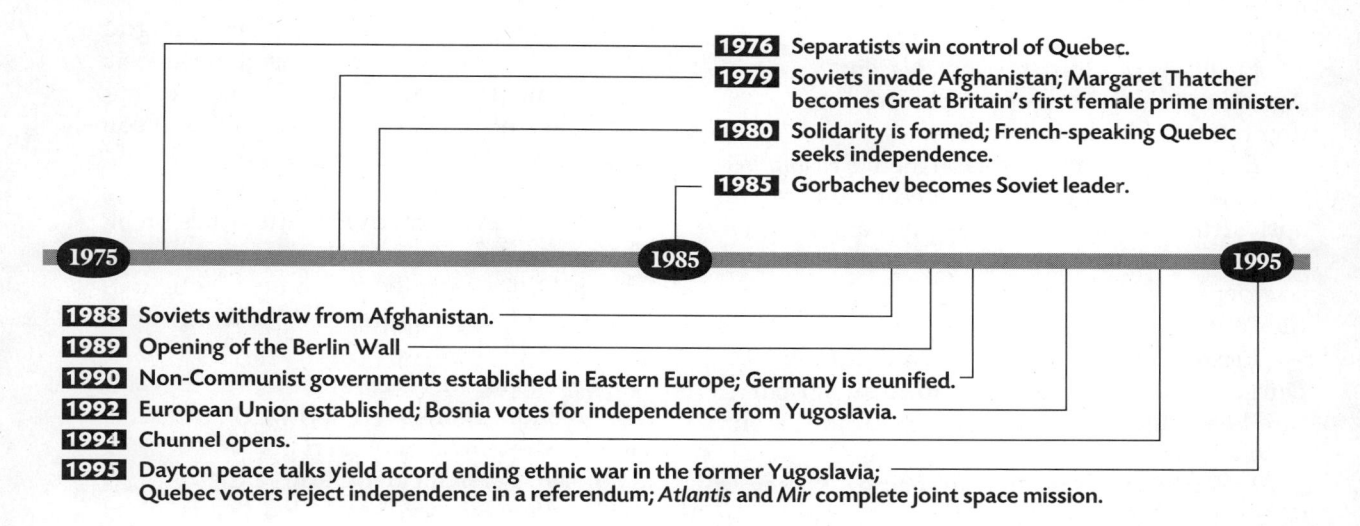

1976 Separatists win control of Quebec.
1979 Soviets invade Afghanistan; Margaret Thatcher becomes Great Britain's first female prime minister.
1980 Solidarity is formed; French-speaking Quebec seeks independence.
1985 Gorbachev becomes Soviet leader.

1975 — 1985 — 1995

1988 Soviets withdraw from Afghanistan.
1989 Opening of the Berlin Wall
1990 Non-Communist governments established in Eastern Europe; Germany is reunified.
1992 European Union established; Bosnia votes for independence from Yugoslavia.
1994 Chunnel opens.
1995 Dayton peace talks yield accord ending ethnic war in the former Yugoslavia; Quebec voters reject independence in a referendum; *Atlantis* and *Mir* complete joint space mission.

Country	Date	Event	Effect or Significance
1. Canada	1980		
2. Baltic states	1990		
3. Germany	1989		
4. Afghanistan	1988		
5. Yugoslavia	1992		
6. Poland	1980		

World History — Time Line Activities

ANSWERS

Time Line Activity 1, p. 1
Answers may vary. Possible answers:
Technology:
   Event: World population reaches 90 million. *Reason:* Improvements in skills and tools result in increased food supplies, which enable many more people to survive.
Domestication:
   Event: Agriculture begins. *Reason:* Agriculture is a result of people learning to domesticate plants and animals.
   Event: Çatal Hüyük established. *Reason:* With the development of domesticated foods and agriculture, people can create permanent homes in villages, such as Çatal Hüyük, rather than wander in search of food.
Civilization:
   Event: Neolithic period occurs. *Reason:* During this period, people shift to an agriculture-based lifestyle, which lays the foundation for civilization.
   Event: Sumerians build first cities. *Reason:* Civilization arises with the building of the first cities.

Time Line Activity 2, p. 2
1. 1700 B.C.; 1000 B.C.
2. 2300 B.C.
3. New Kingdom
4. Indus River valley
5. 3000 B.C.
6. 1000 B.C.
7. 500
8. 1100
9. 3100 B.C.
10. 1800

Time Line Activity 3, p. 3
Cultural Diffusion:
   Event: Aramaeans control rich overland trade between Egypt and Mesopotamia. *Explanation:* Because the Aramaean caravans crossed and recrossed the Fertile Crescent on business, people throughout the region learned Aramaic.
Innovation:
   Event: Abraham makes a covenant with God; monotheism created. *Explanation:* The belief in one all-powerful God was an exception among the polythestic cultures of the ancient world.
   Event: Assyrian Empire reaches its height. *Explanation:* Assyrians had the most lethal fighting force in the Middle East to subdue rebellions. They also built a network of roads to improve communication.
   Event: Lydians develop a money system using coins. *Explanation:* The Lydian kingdom, Asia Minor, was famous for its gold deposits; coins came to replace barter. Soon Greek and Persian rulers began to stamp their own coins, and the concept of money spread.
Conflict:
   Event: Ten northern Israelite tribes break away from two southern tribes. *Explanation:* The Israelites resented Solomon's high taxes and harsh labor requirements; after his death, the tribes broke away.
   Event: Assyrians conquer Israel. *Explanation:* The two kingdoms were too weak to resist invasion by the powerful Assyrians.
   Event: Persian ruler Darius I dies. *Explanation:* His son Xerxes led Persia in a disastrous campaign to conquer Greece in 480 B.C., crippling the Persian Empire.

Time Line Activity 4, p. 4
1. *Answers will vary. Possible answer:* The farther you go back in history, the less likely you are to find written records or other artifacts preserved.
2. approximately 443 years
3. just after 1100 B.C.
4. 621 B.C.
5. 33 years

Time Line Activity 5, p. 5
1. 24 years
2. Philip II's reign
3. Hippocrates
4. the opening of the Lyceum
5. Hippocrates

Time Line Activity 6, p. 6
1. F—Since patricians engraved laws in 451 B.C. and plebeians did not win right to make laws until 287 B.C., patricians clearly had more power.

2. F—Plebeians gained the right to make laws in 287 B.C., but in 146 B.C., Rome burned Carthage, indicating that relations between Rome and Carthage were not peaceful.
3. T—Rome burned Carthage in 146 B.C. and Julius Caesar was assassinated in 44 B.C. Since it is unlikely that he ruled for 102 years, he clearly came to power after the defeat of Carthage.
4. F—Augustus was Rome's first emperor.
5. T—Augustus took power in 27 B.C. and the *Pax Romana* ended in 180 A.D., which is a total of 207 years.
6. T—Jesus was crucified in A.D. 33, and Christianity became the official religion of Rome in A.D. 392, 359 years later.

Time Line Activity 7, p. 7

1. about 900 years
2. 500 B.C.
3. 53 years
4. c. A.D. 1324
5. Christianity became the kingdom's official religion.
6. A.D. 1475
7. Axum
8. Arab and Persian merchants came and settled along East Africa's coast, thus introducing their culture.

Time Line Activity 8, p. 8

Students' matches between concepts and events will vary but should include an explanation for their answers. Possible answers:
  Unity: Aryans invade northern India—the Aryans introduced Sanskrit and the *varna* system, both of which helped create a system of government
  Innovation: Aryans invade northern India—the creation of the Aryan epics and the Vedas
  Conflict: Aryans invade northern India—Aryans conquered native people living in India when they arrived
  Unity: Vedic Age—the Vedas describe how the Aryan social system organized society
  Innovation: Vedic Age—the Vedas represent the earliest written form of Sanskrit discovered
  Unity: Upanishads written—the *Upanishads* represent religious agreement, formed over many centuries, about rebirth and the soul
  Innovation: Upanishads written—the *Upanishads* were used by later dynasties, such as the Guptas, to set up an educational system
  Unity: Chandragupta Maurya—his dynasty lasted for almost 150 years
  Innovation: Chandragupta Maurya—set up postal service; good administrator
  Conflict: Chandragupta Maurya—built his kingdom on conquests; possessed many spies and soldiers
  Innovation: Ajanta caves decorated by monks—cave paintings from Ajanta eventually influenced Buddhist art throughout Asia
  Unity: Chandragupta II rules Gupta Empire—lowered taxes on his people; Sanskrit became official language of northern India
  Innovation: Chandragupta II rules Gupta Empire—flowering of literature, poetry, and science
  Conflict: Chandragupta II rules Gupta Empire—women lost certain rights

Time Line Activity 9, p. 9

Zhou Dynasty:
  Events: origins of Confucianism and Daoism
  Life: Philosophical and literary traditions of later dynasties begin.
Qin Dynasty:
  Events: Great Wall built; book burning; standardized written language
  Life: Answers should demonstrate a clear understanding of the unifying effects of Shihuangdi's rule, as well as the personal hardships suffered by many of his subjects.
Han Dynasty:
  Events: Zhang Qian travels as far as Rome; Han armies defeat enemies; Sima Qian writes *Historical Records*; Confucian schools established;
Pax Sinica:
  Life: Answers should link the pacification of the Han's foreign enemies and the establishment of trade with far-flung nations with the incredible period of peace and artistic development that followed.

Time Line Activity 10, p. 10

1. 1123 years
2. A.D. 860
3. A.D. 1204
4. 57 years
5. Yaroslav
6. 165 years
7. A.D. 726
8. c. A.D. 860

Time Line Activity 11, p. 11
1. A.D. 786; Abbasid
2. A.D. 630
3. A.D. 732; Umayyad
4. death of Muhammad
5. A.D. 622
6. A.D. 750
7. A.D. 610
8. Ma'mun; A.D. 830
9. A.D. 656
10. A.D. 680

Time Line Activity 12, p. 12
1. Otto the Great
2. William the Conqueror
3. *Answers should include the signing of the Magna Carta, which reduced the power of the king.*
4. the Inquisition
5. Concordat of Worms
6. Philip Augustus

Time Line Activity 13, p. 13
1. universities
2. 72 years
3. the Hundred Years' War
4. 19 years old
5. battle of Crécy and battle of Agincourt
6. Jan Hus
7. Wars of the Roses

Time Line Activity 14, p. 14
1. China and Vietnam
2. during the A.D. 1100s
3. Genghis Khan's armies under his grandson, Kublai Khan, overthrew the Song dynasty and set up the Yuan dynasty in China.
4. 897 years
5. Korea; Yi; A.D. 1392
6. moderate—53 years

Time Line Activity 15, p. 15
1. 5
2. Olmec, Teotihuacáno, Toltec
3. They lived in different areas of Mesoamerica.
4. It was the earliest known civilization of Mesoamerica.
5. The only assumption one could make is that the two civilizations had some contact. Although the Maya began before the Toltec, they overlapped in time. Therefore, it would be unclear whether the design originated with the Toltec or the Maya.

Time Line Activity 16, p. 16
1. Johannes Gutenberg creates first printing press.
2. Desiderius Erasmus writes *The Praise of Folly*.
3. Martin Luther nails theses to door of Wittenberg Church.
4. the Wars of the Roses, which did not end until 1485
5. the Inquisition
6. 102 years
7. John Calvin

Time Line Activity 17, p. 17
1. 3 years
2. 3 years
3. 148 years
4. 1534
5. the English; Jamestown

Time Line Activity 18, p. 18
1. Abdul-Mejid I
2. The first Ottoman parliament met; the sultan ended constitutional rule. (*This information should be added at 1877.*)
3. Akbar became the ruler of India in 1556.
4. Qing; Manchus (*This information should be added at 1644.*)
5. Christians defy authorities and are attacked. (*This information should be added at 1637.*)

Time Line Activity 19, p. 19
1. her cousin, Mary Stuart
2. 1618
3. *Possible responses:* Protestant rebellion; religious freedom
4. Portugal
5. *Possible response:* Europe during this time period was a place of great social and political upheaval and violence.

Time Line Activity 20, p. 20
Science/Mathematics:
   Event: Newton publishes his book *Principia*. *Significance:* Offered a new understanding of planetary motion, building on the work of Copernicus, Galileo, and Kepler; developed calculus.
Government/Politics:
   Event: Locke publishes his *Two Treatises of Government*; Maria Theresa rules Austria; Frederick II rules Prussia; the American Revolution begins. *Significance:* Locke introduced the idea that government was accountable

to individuals; influenced American patriots. Maria Theresa was influenced by Enlightenment philosophy; introduced measures to free peasants, protect serfs, and provide public education. Frederick II tried to apply political ideals of the Enlightenment. The American Revolution used Enlightenment notions of individual rights as the basis for revolting against British rule.
Philosophy/Religion:
   Event: The Enlightenment occurs; Diderot publishes the *Encyclopédie*; Rousseau's *Discourse on the Effect of the Arts and Sciences on Morals* makes him famous. *Significance:* The Enlightenment spread the ideas of the scientific revolution and applied a scientific approach to areas previously defined by religion. The *Encyclopédie* criticized the Church and government and spread ideas of religious tolerance throughout Europe. Rousseau's *Discourse* asserted the limitations of reason and the value of instinct and emotion in human life.
The Arts:
   Event: Romantic movement occurs. *Significance:* Artists broke with classicism to celebrate emotion and the individual.

Time Line Activity 21, p. 21
1. English Bill of Rights, George Washington becomes first president
2. five
3. 1770
4. 1653
5. 22 years
6. George III
7. six
8. It was repealed after only one year.
9. 11

Time Line Activity 22, p. 22
Students should mark the fall of the Bastille in 1789, Napoleon's coup d'état in 1799, the Battle of Waterloo in 1815, and Napoleon's naming of himself as Emperor of France in 1804 on their time lines.
1. a. the fall of the Bastille in 1789
   b. 9 years
2. a. Napoleon's coup d'état in 1799
   b. the Battle of Waterloo in 1815
3. He named himself Emperor of France in 1804.
4. *Answers will vary, but should be supported with explanations. The original noble goals of the National Assembly deteriorate into the Reign of Terror within two years; less than a decade later, France is ruled by a dictator.*

Time Line Activity 23, p. 23
1. the invention of the seed drill; it made planting more efficient
2. stockings, thread, nails
3. Weavers couldn't keep up with the production of thread. Cartwright's power loom solved this problem. *Students should add the invention of the power loom at 1787.*
4. Cities were becoming larger. As cities grew, there was a need for more specific addresses, so houses were numbered. As cities grew, there was more traffic. Paved sidewalks kept people out of the way of carriages and other vehicles.
5. *Changes in transportation include:* canal between Liverpool and Leeds; first iron bridge; horse-drawn wagon on rails; steam locomotive. *Students' additions will vary. Possible answers:* 1801, steam-powered carriage; 1807, steamboat

Time Line Activity 24, p. 24
1. 60
2. All deal with objects that can be seen only with a microscope.
3. People realized that things that appear solid and seamless are actually made of tiny invisible units of matter.
4. 72
5. *Answers will vary. Some students may argue that it reflects Smith's philosophy since, if labor is the source of a nation's wealth, an educated workforce should create more wealth. Others may feel that it reflects Marx's goals, since making education available to all is a step toward removing class distinctions. Any answers are acceptable as long as they demonstrate an understanding of a basic tenet of one of the economic theories described in this chapter.*

Time Line Activity 25, p. 25
1. the Reform Act
2. 3 years
3. 50 years
4. the signing of the Treaty of Waitangi
5. 67 years

Time Line Activity 26, p. 26

Nationalism/Reform: 1815 Creation of German Confederation; 1861 Alexander II frees Russian serfs; 1861 Victor Emmanuel II becomes king of a united Italy; 1863 Lassalle forms Universal German Workingmen's Association; 1867 Austria and Hungary form dual monarchy; 1871 William I becomes emperor of a united Germany

Reaction: 1825 the Decembrist uprising is crushed; 1849 Austria reestablishes control of Venetia; 1861 Alexander II frees Russian serfs; 1867 Austria and Hungary form dual monarchy; 1905 Nicholas II dissolves the duma; 1913 Ottoman Empire attacks Bulgaria in Balkan conflict

Time Line Activity 27, p. 27

Answers will vary. Answers may include any five of the following:

Event: Great Britain wins the Opium War. *Type of Influence:* Economic. *Explanation:* Unequal treaties took economic advantage of the Chinese.

Event: Commodore Perry reaches Japan. *Type of Influence:* Economic. *Explanation:* Japan trades with other countries.

Event: Indian Revolt occurs. *Type of Influence:* Social. *Explanation:* Sepoys resented British attempts to impose Christianity and European customs on Indian culture.

Event: Suez Canal opens. *Type of Influence:* Economic. *Explanation:* Travel time between Europe and Asia is shortened.

Event: Fourteen European nations meet to partition Africa. *Type of Influence:* Economic. *Explanation:* All African countries except Liberia and Ethiopia were colonies of Europe.

Event: United States wins the Spanish-American War. *Type of Influence:* Economic. *Explanation:* United States gained valuable territories: Philippine Islands, Guam, and Puerto Rico.

Event: Boxer Rebellion occurs. *Type of Influence:* Social. *Explanation:* Boxers wanted to retain Chinese tradition.

Event: Japan wins the Russo-Japanese War. *Type of Influence:* Political. *Explanation:* Japan controlled Korea and nearby areas.

Event: Panama Canal opens. *Type of Influence:* Economic. *Explanation:* Shorter route between Atlantic and Pacific Oceans is created.

Time Line Activity 28, p. 28

Answers may vary. Possible answers:
Cooperation:

Event: France and Russia sign military alliance; Entente Cordiale between France and Great Britain. *Explanation:* Alliance brings together countries to support one another against aggressors.

Event: President Wilson asks Congress to declare war to help Allies. *Explanation:* United States assists the Allied Powers.

Event: Signing of Treaty of Versailles. *Explanation:* Big Four work together to bring about peace agreement.
Conflict:

Event: Balkan Wars. *Explanation:* fighting for control of Ottoman territory

Event: Assassination of Archduke Francis Ferdinand. *Explanation:* event that sparked the war

Event: Austria-Hungary declares war on Serbia. *Explanation:* beginning of war

Event: Germans invade Belgium. *Explanation:* beginning of conflict along the Western Front

Event: France and Germany fight the Battle of the Marne. *Explanation:* major battle

Event: Allied defeat at Gallipoli. *Explanation:* Turks fight back against Allies.

Event: President Wilson asks Congress to declare war to help Allies. *Explanation:* United States enters war to defeat the Central Powers.

Event: Germans sign armistice. *Explanation:* end of German war effort

Event: Signing of Treaty of Versailles. *Explanation:* Terms for Germany are harsh; Germany becomes resentful and angry.
Revolution:

Event: Assassination of Archduke Francis Ferdinand. *Explanation:* Assassins try to throw Austrians out of Bosnia.

Event: Coup d'état topples provisional government in Russia. *Explanation:* This was a backlash against the provisional government's attempt to take control from the czar.

Event: Civil war in Russia. *Explanation:* Bolsheviks fight to take over government.

Event: Russia's White armies admit defeat. *Explanation:* Communists complete their revolution.
Internationalism:

Event: Wilson presents Fourteen Points. *Explanation:* original plan for greater international stability; League of Nations idea introduced

Event: Signing of Treaty of Versailles. Explanation: Along with other peace treaties, right of self-determination given to new nations; war ended through international agreement.

Time Line Activity 29, p. 29
1. 1920
2. 14 years
3. 1935
4. a. Italy
   b. Mussolini
5. a. stock market crash
   b. 1929
6. 1922
7. 1933

Time Line Activity 30, p. 30
Asia: 1917, Balfour Declaration; 1919, Amritsar Massacre; 1925, Chiang Kai-shek sets up government at Nanjing; 1930, Prime Minister Osachi Hamaguchi assassinated; 1930, Mohandas K. Gandhi leads salt tax march; 1934, Mao Zedong leads the Long March

Africa: 1921, Harry Thuku organizes nationalists; 1937, Nnamdi Azikwe starts a newspaper

Latin America: 1933, Franklin D. Roosevelt announces Good Neighbor policy; 1937, President Getúlio Vargas proclaims a new constitution; 1938, Lázaro Cárdenas nationalizes oil wells

Time Line Activity 31, p. 31
1. 1940; Germans enter Paris and France surrenders.
2. 1945; United States drops atomic bombs on Hiroshima and Nagasaki.
3. 1936; Spanish Civil War begins.
4. 1941; Japan attacks U.S. naval base at Pearl Harbor.
5. 1938; *Anschluss* plan to group all German peoples into one country is put into action.
6. 1943; Allies invade island of Sicily.

Time Line Activity 32, p. 32
1945: Cooperative effort—United Nations formed.
1946: Conflict—Churchill delivers his "iron curtain" speech.
1947: Cooperative effort—Truman Doctrine and Marshall Plan initiated.
1948: Conflict—Soviets blockade Berlin; Cooperative Effort—United States launches airlift.
1949: Cooperative effort—NATO formed.
1955: Cooperative effort—Warsaw Pact formed.
1956: Conflict: Khrushchev delivers de-Stalinization speech; Soviets crush uprisings in Hungary.
1960: Conflict—U-2 incident heightens cold war tensions.
1961: Conflict—Berlin Wall erected.
1968: Conflict—Soviets invade Czechoslovakia.

Time Line Activity 33, p. 33
1. 1950
2. 36
3. 24
4. 21
5. 19
6. 4
7. 1972
8. 34
9. 1964
10. 2

Time Line Activity 34, p. 34
1. Sudan
2. 1960
3. 11 years
4. Jomo Kenyatta's presidency
5. the period from the introduction of apartheid to the outbreak of riots

Time Line Activity 35, p. 35
1. 10 (events in 1948, 1956, 1964, 1967, 1973, 1980, 1982, 1987, 1990, 1995)
2. 4 (events in 1945, 1979, 1993, 1994)
3. *Answers will vary. Possible answer:* Although there are more events leading to conflict, the steps toward peace have occurred more recently.

Time Line Activity 36, p. 36
1. Batista, 1959, Cuba; Allende, 1973, Chile; Somoza, 1979, Nicaragua; Aristide, 1991, Haiti
2. 3 years; Cuban missile crisis
3. 15 years; Pinochet
4. *Students should add* 1992—Panama's Manuel Noriega convicted of drug trafficking charges *to the time line.*

5. El Salvador; 12 years
6. *Students should add* 1990—Violeta Chamorro elected Nicaraguan president *to the time line.*

Time Line Activity 37, p. 37
Answers will vary. Possible answers:
1. French-speaking Quebec seeks independence; soon after, new constitution gives more power to provinces, protects language and cultural rights.
2. Baltic republics declared independence; started breakup of Soviet Union.
3. Opening of Berlin Wall; reunification of Germany soon follows.
4. Soviet troops withdraw; sign of easing of cold war
5. Bosnia votes for independence; war breaks out in Bosnia.
6. Solidarity is formed; Walesa becomes symbol of freedom throughout Eastern Europe.